The Hay-Wagon
by Abigail Olson

ABIGAIL OLSON

THE HAY-
WAGON

a memoir

BELLE ISLE BOOKS
www.belleislebooks.com

ISBN: 978-1-951565-30-5
LCCN: 2020910375

Printed in the United States of America

Published by
Belle Isle Books (an imprint of Brandylane Publishers, Inc.)
5 S. 1st Street
Richmond, Virginia 23219

BELLE ISLE BOOKS
www.belleislebooks.com

belleislebooks.com | brandylanepublishers.com

For every "Gatlin" and the girls who dated him

All names have been changed.

Contents

Kind of Fluent

"*¿Eres mexicana?*"

"*No.*"

"*Entonces, ¿cómo aprendiste español?*"

"*Pues, cuando tenía uno a cinco años, fui a una escuela del nombre Mi Escuelita, y las maestras eran de Colombia. Nos hablaron solamente en español.*" [Todavía no sé como decir "Spanish-immersion preschool" en español.][1]

---

[1] "Are you Mexican?"

"No."

"So how did you learn Spanish?"

"Well, when I was one to five, I went to a school named Mi Escuelita, and the teachers were from Colombia. They only spoke to us in Spanish." [I still don't know how to say "Spanish-immersion preschool" in Spanish.]

Highway Horn

"Hey, Abigail, watch this."

I turned to watch Waylon as he pumped his fist up and down near the car window. Around five years old, I didn't know what I was supposed to watch for until I heard it: a blasting highway horn from a passing semi.

Back then, I didn't know the term "highway horn" or that trucks also had city horns or that the motion Waylon did was the exact same motion the driver had to do to make that incredulous sound.

I couldn't even see the driver, but I wondered about him. And about Waylon. How did Waylon know to pump his fist? And when? And how did he know the driver would see? And that the driver would respond? The driver was way up there, above our little car. He *saw* Waylon. He *responded* to Waylon. And he didn't have to, either.

In my mind, the driver was basically Santa Claus, an old man way up high that looked in every car window for a little boy pumping his fist and proceeded to deliver joy. Two strangers passing on a highway had a connection. I wanted that.

Afton Mountain

What could possibly be taking so long? I thought, anxious to start up the mountain.

Every year, my family has a reunion at our summer vacation place, a mountaintop we share. On Saturday night, we ride the hay-wagon to the top. The adults can walk and drive up, too. We have a cookout and play yard games and make s'mores. Then we come back down the mountain for a talent show.

It all starts with the ride up, though, and even after all the kids got in, the adults liked to dilly-dally. There were a group of men—uncles, cousins—huddled by the truck that pulled the hay-wagon. I couldn't make out what they said, but it seemed very important. So important, in fact, that it held up the entire operation. This happened every year, and we didn't go until they said so. Looking back, we were probably waiting for a cousin that still had some food to place into the wagon or games to throw in the back. Or maybe someone had to use the restroom quickly.

Whatever the reason, I knew that the real ones in charge were up front. They made the calls. When they climbed into the truck—even the bed, which was so way cool—that meant we could go. Maybe one day, they'd let me be up in the truck with them. Maybe even the passenger seat up front.

Shock Collar

I'd just started school in Richmond, so my mother and I tried to reconnect with our extended family living there. One evening, I found myself surrounded by aunts and uncles on my uncle's porch.

Our host—my aunt—and another family member rocked back and forth on the porch swing while the rest of us perched ourselves on the railing. Around nine years old, I tuned in and out of the adult conversation.

An aunt started talking about a new shock collar they got to train their dog. "I was really worried that it'd hurt the dog, but then I heard that you're supposed to shock yourself on the wrist to feel the pain that the dog would feel. And then you can adjust the shock intensity if it's too much or too little."

"So, did you?" a voice asked. I didn't know my family well enough yet to distinguish who said what.

"Yeah, yeah, we did."

"What was it like?"

"It was definitely scary but not too bad."

Somehow the conversation turned my way. "Abigail, try it."

"What?"

"Put the collar on your wrist. You can see what the dog feels when it tries to cross the invisible fence."

"I'm okay."

"No, just try it. It's not that bad. Right?" An uncle turned to another uncle.

"Yeah, yeah. We can put it on the lowest setting. See?"

"No, thanks." Although I was flattered by the sudden attention they were giving me, why would I shock myself on purpose? I didn't try to cross the fence, and I wasn't a dog. I didn't buy the collar for my dog to be shocked, and they already had the shock level all figured out anyway.

"Look, I'll do it on myself. And then you can do it." My uncle didn't react when he shocked himself. "See? That's how not painful it is. Try it."

He tried to hand me the collar. I didn't take it. "That's okay." I didn't know too much about electricity, but maybe it would affect me differently than it had him since he was bigger. I didn't know, and I didn't want to risk it.

A sea of faces told me it'd be okay. It wasn't a big deal. Just try it. Look, they all did it. It was on the lowest setting.

I kept shaking my head and smiling. At one point, the collar came to a rest on my left wrist. All I had to do was push the button. My right hand hovered over it. They *were* all fine. . . . They wouldn't intentionally put me in harm's way. . . . After all, I *was* starting to get curious about what the shock felt like. . . .

No! I didn't want to do it in the beginning, and I didn't want to do it now. None of the facts had changed, so I handed back the shock collar.

When my mother and I drove home that night, she was furious, and I didn't understand why. My aunts and uncles hadn't done anything wrong. They didn't force me to shock myself, and I didn't even end up pushing the button anyway. Why was my mom all worked up?

"You know, I grew up with your uncle, and he knows how to put on the peer pressure. I've never seen anyone not give in to him."

"I just didn't want to."

Third Home

My dad and I had just gotten back from the store, and we sat on the porch a little before two-thirty to wait for my mother. The first sip of cream soda, an extra special treat, bubbled in my mouth just as her white car pulled up.

"She's not supposed to be here until three."

"Bye, Dad. I love you!" I gave him a quick hug and kiss, rushing to make sure my parents wouldn't exchange even a glance. Under no circumstance would I allow the two worlds to collide.

After shutting the car door and sliding into the middle of the backseat, I said, "Mom! Why are you early? My dad and I were gonna drink cream soda."

"It's almost a three-hour drive from Richmond to Hillsboro. I have to allow time for traffic."

"It's okay. Mom! Where are the Cheetos I left on Friday? I was going to eat them on the way to South Hill."

"Oops, I ate them. I didn't realize you were saving them."

Great. No cream soda and no Cheetos. I'd have to wait until we stopped at the Exxon at Exit 12B. South Hill, the halfway point. Maybe I could use it as leverage to get *two* bags of chips.

Until then, I made myself comfortable. Still too young to sit up front, I sat in the middle of the backseat so I could reach forward and change the CDs. My two favorites were the ones with the songs from *Les Misérables*. Sometimes, I'd mix it up with a country or children's CD.

I could be in the car for hours. I didn't have to talk to anyone. I could listen to whatever I wanted. I could eat pretty much whatever I wanted. I felt at peace during those two three-hour car rides every month. They started when I turned eight and my mother moved to Richmond. After my dad moved to Wisconsin when I was ten, I joked that the Chicago O'Hare airport had become my new "third home," replacing the car.

A.A.

On the heels of my middle school's Drug and Alcohol Night, my mother took me to an A.A. meeting. She felt my school lacked the ability to realistically portray alcoholism and its effects. One of my grandfathers died of the disease, and the other got sober two years before he died.

We sat in the car and watched for someone we could follow in.

"Usually, meetings are in some random back location that are hard to find unless you know where you're going," my mother said as we scanned the parking lot.

The meeting ended up being in the middle of the third floor of a church. I barely knew churches had second floors, let alone third ones.

"This meeting is open, which means it is open to the public," Mom said. "Anyone who is curious or wants to learn about A.A. is welcome. Closed meetings are for members only."

"Why would one be closed?"

"A lot of the members have tough stories, and sometimes it's easier to be more vulnerable and share when only other alcoholics are present. But this meeting has a speaker. It'll be one person sharing their story the whole time instead of going around the room."

The speaker stood at a podium in the front of the small room. My mother and I sat in the back row. I listened, drifting in and out of the speaker's story. God played a big role in the person's life, except God wasn't called "God" but "a Higher Power."

My mother explained, "Churches can be alienating for some people, and not everyone believes in the same religion, so to be inclusive and accessible for everyone, A.A. and Al-Anon have what's called a Higher Power. It can be anything the person wants as long as it is bigger than they are and takes the focus off of themselves. It could be a mountain, a thunderstorm, a doorknob, the God from a specific religion, angels, the universe, anything."

Everyone in that room seemed so grounded, like they'd been through so much, but kind of in a good way, somehow. I couldn't explain how or why, but I wanted to be like them, just without the whole "hitting rock bottom" and "disease of alcoholism" part. My mother told me the only requirement for membership is to want to stop drinking. Too young to have drunk alcohol, I didn't promise myself I'd never, ever drink my whole entire life, but I do think of that moment every time I'm offered a drink, and I have yet to take a sip of alcohol.

Personality Test

Walking to lower and middle school, I'd pass by the back entrance of the country club on my street. Despite the fact that I'd heard many wonderful things about the club, the sight of huge dumpsters and the smell of rotten eggs always came to mind first. Rather than the five pools or three golf courses, my next most common associations were the semis on my narrow street backing into the kitchen entrance.

"Give them plenty of space. Wait, be patient," my mother always told me.

I'd watch from a distance as the drivers backed in at a rather complicated angle. Some got frustrated. Some asked for guidance. Some did it smoothly, hardly even blinking. Some pulled out and in countless times, and others backed in with one move.

How did they know what to do? When to turn the wheel? How quickly? What could the club need so much of? What would happen if the drivers couldn't back in? Would someone else be able to do it, or was the entire operation riding on them and their abilities?

—

In eighth grade, we took a career personality test. It ranked hundreds of possible jobs and how well they fit my character. Each career had a red or green bar beside it; all green totally fit and all red totally did not. Since there were so many options, I could search individual results. Thinking of those drivers at the back entrance of the club, I searched "truck driver."

Could I do what they did? Could I navigate narrow twists and turns with a huge trailer?

Positive match! Not super positive, but somewhat. That counted. Better than negative, at least.

A Common "Horror" Story

The summer vacation before junior year, my friends and I sat on a porch, eating pizza off paper plates and talking about sex and marriage and boys.

"Well, *I* know to actually wait all the way until marriage," said one of the girls. "One girl in my Sunday school had a boyfriend, and she thought they were going to get married, so they had sex. She thought it was okay, but then they broke up. She's had a really hard time."

This cautionary tale had a moral. We would be smarter and learn from that girl's mistake. We knew then not to trust boys, even though we loved them, and to wait until marriage for sex. Why? I wasn't sure, but I understood in my friend's tone that sex before marriage was not okay. That other girl had been tricked. And then she was devastated. All because of sex before marriage? I hadn't known my position on when sex was appropriate, but I decided maybe I should wait for marriage. Just to be safe.

But then again, almost nobody did that anyway . . . so maybe I wouldn't wait *all* the way until marriage. Or maybe I *would* wait. . . . The decision just seemed so stressful.

Earthquake Drill

Junior year. Physics class. Earthquake drill. Under tables. Chat time!

"Abigail, I did so bad on that calc test. How did you do?"

"Oh, yeah, that? I got a C, so I tried to drop out, but then our teacher tried to talk me out of it. And he asked where I wanted to go to college, so I said I wanted to be a truck driver, and yeah, now I'm staying in BC for some reason."

"Abi, be real. You're not really going to be a truck driver."

The audacity! She was right, though. How serious was I actually? Did I enjoy just throwing it out there but not committing to it yet? Why shouldn't I become one? In that moment, I decided to commit to the fantasy. All my friends would be able to say they had a trucker friend. That'd be so cool.

"Yes, I am. Watch me."

Car Crash

"Hi, this is Malone."

"Hi, Malone. This is Abigail Olson. I was just calling to see if I could sign up to get my commercial driver's license?"

"Yes, yes. Just come by before you start."

"Great! Thank you so much. I'll come by the week before? I'd like to do the Monday through Friday class."

"Okay."

I called 7 Sons CDL Training about six weeks before my senior year ended. Two weeks later, I crashed my car. Completely my fault.

A line of cars was parked in front of a gas station, making it hard to see traffic coming from the right. A woman in the lane closest to the sidewalk waved me out. I turned right into the far lane instead of the close one and ran into someone else's car. My mother always told me not to listen to people waving me on. The person I'd hit and I parked in the middle of the road.

I called my mother. She told me to drive my car to the side of the road so I wouldn't block traffic. Then the other woman used my phone to call her husband, who came with a whole gang of people.

My mother arrived, and I cried. I couldn't become a truck driver anymore. What would I do with my life now?

"Do you know that for sure?" My mother asked.

"No."

"Who can you ask?"

"Malone?"

"Then call him."

"Can I call him now?"

"If you want to."

I called Malone. "Hi, Malone. Um, if I crashed, can I still become a truck driver? Can I still get my CDL?"

"Well, obviously, you don't want too many crashes. But one or two every few years is okay, I'd say."

"Oh, okay. Thank you, thank you! Yes, it's only this one."

Sometimes, the best way to learn is to crash.

Registration

When I walked into the 7 Sons building, a bulletin board hanging on the wall caught my eye. It hadn't filled up yet, and I looked at each picture carefully. These were the students who'd passed their CDL test and who now occupied the highways. How many women? How many young people? How many young women? Everyone was grinning. They were proud. Maybe if I passed, my picture could be there, too.

I wandered toward an office door and knocked softly. "Come in."

Finally face to face with Malone, I sat in his office.

"Do you have your learner's permit?" he asked.

"Yeah! I have my license." Wow, I was already ahead of the game.

"Then why are you here?"

"Wait, what? I have my driver's license."

"You need a CDL learner's permit. We'll show you how to get that."

"Okay."

"Class A, B, or C?"

"What?" I laughed nervously. Already way in over my head.

"B is for straight trucks like dump trucks or school buses. A also includes tractor-trailers."

My friend's dad's advice came back to me: *Get your license to drive everything. And don't let it expire. You'll be surprised how many situations come up when you'll be the only one who can drive something.*

"Class A, I think."

I signed the paperwork. I'd need to get a DOT physical, then read the DMV manual to pass the three written tests for a permit.

As we walked out, Malone shook my hand and gestured to my shorts. They were *really* short. Eva had picked them out for me to wear at a fraternity party we had gone to together. She loved to show off my long, strong legs.

"Maybe wear sweatpants and sneakers. . . . Wouldn't want them to say anything to you, but I can't control them. . . ."

I get to wear sweatpants? I chose the right career after all!

Getting Started

The Monday after my high school's Friday graduation ceremony, I showed up more than nervous to my first day of CDL training. There were a few people sitting at a picnic table on raised pavement, while two trucks backed up and pulled forward. I couldn't tell what anyone was doing. Would I even be allowed in a truck? How would I know how to turn the wheel and when? And there were so many orange cones! Maybe this wasn't right for me. I didn't even know how to get in!

The students watched other students practice backing maneuvers as I walked up.

I watched a man, also a little unsure, approach an instructor. "No English," he said.

I turned around to look at another instructor. Was this guy for real? He was going to learn everything without knowing English? The instructor I turned to explained, "That's Feng. Today's his first day, too. He's from China. We'll see how this goes."

Relief washed over me. I admired Feng's confidence. If he was ready to tackle this challenge, I was ready, too, and at least I knew English.

An instructor used hand motions to direct Feng, and I watched as he got into the truck and backed up straight. He did it perfectly and quickly. The instructors were impressed. One of them explained to me the difficulty of backing up with a trailer, "It's like pushing something with the front wheel of a wheelbarrow. It goes back and forth, so you gotta turn the wheel, even if you're tryna go straight."

When Feng got out of the truck, one of the instructors motioned a bit more. "Understand?"

Feng nodded and climbed back in. He drove the truck forward and backed it into the next lane over.

The instructor turned to me and said, "Oh, he's done this before."

"How do you know?"

"That's an offset. It usually takes days or weeks to learn. He just did it perfectly without a single pull-up."

"What's a pull-up?"

"When you have to go forward."

"Is that bad?"

"It's . . . okay. You can't do any for the straight back, and you can have one for the offset."

"And that over there?" I pointed to the other truck, which a driver was maneuvering.

"Parallel parking. That's after you get the offset."

"How many pull-ups do you get for that?"

"Two."

"What happens if I can't do these things in those amounts of pull-ups?"

"You can't get more than twelve points or you fail. One point for each pull-up you do over what's allowed and two points if you hit a cone."

The instructor downloaded the Google Translator app to communicate with Feng. As it turned out, Feng had been a truck driver in China and came to Virginia to get his CDL because it was easier to drive in the United States without all the traffic.

"Alright, Miss Abigail. Your turn."

"Mine?"

"Yup."

"I don't know. . . ."

"Look, it's easy. Always have at least three points of contact going up and down. You can use this grab bar next to the door and the steps and the wheel. One, two, three. Do that, and you get in. Like, two feet and a hand on the wheel or something. Got it?"

"Okay."

"Remember: steer toward the fear."

"What?"

"The ass-end of the trailer goes the opposite way you turn the wheel. So, when you're scared to run into the cones, turn the wheel toward the cones."

"Okay, and so what do I do?"

"Just go forward, and then come back. Don't hit any cones."

Right foot on the first step, right hand on the grab bar, left foot on the second step. Left hand reached up to grab the wheel as my right foot stepped into the cab, right hand still on the bar. Butt in seat, close the door, look to instructor. Instructor nodded. Wow, I was so cool.

Okay. Right hand on the stick. It went all the way to the floor.

"Wait! You know how to drive stick?"

"Yeah, my car is stick."

"Reverse is up front. Stay in first gear, below reverse, and release slow, slow when you reverse. Don't need to use the accelerator."

"Got it."

I tried to put the truck in first gear, but all I heard were grinding noises. I pushed the clutch in farther. More grinding noises.

"Open the door."

The instructor stuck his head in through the open door.

"Slowly release the clutch."

The gears caught, and I was off. Instructor closed the door. I got to the end of the parking lot and looked through my mirrors. I could see the end of the trailer between the two lines of cones. *Just back up slow, adjust when I need to.*

Grr. I ran into a cone. Now the trailer wasn't lined up right.

"Pull up!" I turned my head. "Go all the way up."

I pulled up to the end of the parking lot. Again, and again, and again until I could get it right. Every time. By lunch, I could back straight, usually without a pull-up.

I forgot my lunch, so another student, a sixty-something former hitchhiker from Montgomery, offered me a ride to the corner store where he got his lunch. Two corn dogs, a bag of chips, and a root beer for me. My mother would not have been pleased with my meal.

All the students and some instructors ate lunch together at the picnic table under a tent, where we sat while we waited for others to practice. The guy from Montgomery sat and smoked in a yellow lawn chair he'd brought. Everyone wanted to know why I was there. I'd smile and say, "I don't know. It just seems fun. How about you? Why do you want to be a truck driver?"

"Money." No further explanation needed. We all knew about the driver shortage and rising wages.

That afternoon, I moved onto the offset.

"Yo daddy a trucker?" one of the students asked me.

I shook my head. "He's a doctor."

"You been in a truck before this?"

"This morning."

"That's it? And you this good?"

Oh, yes—trucking was for me after all.

—

Or maybe it wasn't.

"Turn the wheel and count to three, and then back into the other lane."

What? How long should I pause between each count? Do I go onetwothree? Or one . . . two . . . three? Or oooone . . . twooooo . . . threeee . . . ? Or one, two, three? If I turned a beat too long, I'd jackknife. I'd look to the mirrors and only see the white of the trailer. Or one mirror would show cones, but there were so many orange cones. Some were from the lane I'd just come from, and others were from the one I was supposed to go into. There was the green cone in the middle line to help distinguish, but that would be behind the trailer.

Or if I turned a beat too short, I'd have to keep turning the wheel, left . . . right . . . little more right . . . left . . . hit a cone. Pull up. Still not straight.

Where are the cones? Why is it so hot? The windows are all the way down.

Sweatpants had not been a good idea in the Virginia summer heat.

Sometimes, I'd be so lost in the cones and mirrors and trailer that an instructor would point to guide me. And other times, by some miracle, I'd actually make it in! Maybe I'd hit a cone or two or pull up a few times, but I did it! By myself, no help!

It felt like doing a math problem. I knew the general goal and the basic tools to solve the problem. The stress of flipping to the back of the book matched the stress of checking to see if I was in the lines. The gratifying feeling when I'd done it right gave me such a boost of confidence. I could do it again if I had to.

But that first day, I didn't get much of that satisfied feeling. Just a lot of stress and confusion and heat and exhaustion. I really had to engage my arm muscles to turn the wheel.

Soon, I'd be able to turn it with one hand, just not on the first day.

—

That evening, I went into Dick's Sporting Goods to buy some basketball shorts—loose enough to keep me cool and unflattering enough to fend off stares, kind of. When I walked into the store, I couldn't help but notice how comfortable the air conditioning was. How fortunate we are to have it in our daily lives. How fortunate I've been to have grown accustomed to it. How fortunate that it is an assumed luxury in today's society. All these people were walking around the cool store like it was nothing! I just wanted to lay down on the cold tile floor and feel the cold air wash over me. I wanted to relish the air conditioning I had taken for granted all my life. No more sweatpants for me.

—

By the end of the second day, I had the offset figured out. Sometimes it'd take a couple pull-ups, and other times I could get the truck right in. Because my car was still in the shop from the crash, my mother came to pick me up.

"Mom! Would you like to see me do an offset?"

"What's that?"

"It's where I start in that lane, and then go straight, and then turn and back up into the lane right next to it."

"You can do that?"

"Yes!"

"What? Those trucks are massive! Can you even get into one?"

Parallel Parking

"If you listen to me, I'll get you in there exactly right every time."

"I'm just going to sit back and let you figure it out on your own."

"Aim for the second to last cone, and keep the two cones in your mirror!"

"Start turning when the back wheel reaches the first cone."

"Keep going, keep going—nope, you ran into a cone."

As my scratched rims would attest, I used to struggle with parallel parking my car. Add a fifty-three-foot enclosed trailer to the back of the struggle, and that was my summer.

Five instructor voices told me five different things. The more I ran into cones trying to parallel park, the more advice flowed. Eventually, the other students, including ones who'd previously failed the test, started to advise me as well. As I sat in the hot truck, I could feel my frustration mounting until I couldn't even pull forward correctly. Irritation is the key to failure when driving a truck; slip-ups increase as patience decreases.

I stopped the vehicle in its funky position and just lay

my head on the wheel. Now was not the time to feel sorry for myself. I took a deep breath and resolved to finish the maneuver, even if it took all day. I wouldn't worry about all the future times I'd have to do it again. I wouldn't get out and let an instructor do it for me. *Just parallel park the truck this one time. That's all you have to do. Everyone else can wait.*

I took a moment to roll the windows all the way down for fresh air and readjust my seat. It was time to get comfortable. I ignored all the voices and focused on the mirrors, the cones, and the trailer.

I started to pull up and straighten out. One of the guys pointed left, another pointed right, yet another told me to keep going straight, and another held a fist up, the signal to stop. I knew they were just trying to help, but it made me so mad. I couldn't turn left and right and forward and stop all at the same time. And who were they to say anything anyway? One had failed his backing at the DMV, another wasn't even on this maneuver yet. The audacity!

Back wheel at the first cone. Turn into the space. Two back cones in my mirror. Keep going, going, going, almost touched the line. Turn the other way. The drive wheel, attached to the cab, ran right over a cone. Immediately, a sea of fists raised.

"You hit a cone!"

"Come out!"

Duh. Just because I couldn't do the maneuver didn't mean I didn't know to stop and pull up when I hit a cone. What did they think I'd been doing this whole time? Just running over cones for the fun of it and not caring? I wanted to scream.

It's okay. It's not about them. You can do this. It's okay.

I straightened up. Back wheel to the first cone. Turn. Two wheels in driver-side mirror. Almost hit a cone, turn! Turn, turn, turn, *please don't hit the front cone with the drive tire* . . . safe! Turn the other way. . . . Stop before I hit a back cone. Done.

I climbed down, checked the lines. All sides within the cones. Barely. But barely is as good as perfect. I didn't even feel bad for the person who'd have to get out of the crooked mess I'd left.

I walked straight to the bathroom, letting the instructors' voices fall away. I couldn't listen to their advice. Not then. I couldn't hear another student telling me what I did wrong. I just needed space to figure it out on my own.

A tear slipped out just as the door clicked. I studied myself in the mirror: red eyes, dirty face, fly-away hair. I washed my hands in a sink that looked like it'd fall to the floor if I touched it, which explained the "Do NOT LEAN ON SINK" sign. I watched the black water run off my hands. I kind of liked the way the steering wheel would cover my hands with dirt; it felt good to wash it off, refreshing.

I locked eyes with the puffy ones in my reflection. "You are going to do this. This is what you want. You are going out there and doing it one more time. Then you're going home to eat pizza, and you're coming right back out tomorrow morning. You're going to be proud of this."

—

By the time I got back to the practice area, it was my turn again. I climbed into the cab and pulled out of the space. Reverse. Back wheel to first cone, turn. Cones in mirror, straighten up. Back, back, back. Turn. Corner of the trailer skimmed the line. Drive tire barely missed the cone. Turn. Back. Straighten up. Perfect! By some miracle, I did it!

When I got out, all the instructors came over to give me fist bumps as I inspected the lines and cones to double-check I'd actually done it. I smiled.

A Surprise in Trucking Culture

"I gotta leave soon. I got work," a student informed the group.

"What do you do?" I asked. Conversations made waiting between practice sessions more enjoyable.

"Chef at a country club."

"Oh! Which one?"

He told me.

"Oh, yeah, I've been there for a tennis camp once in the summer, but I go to a different one." I told him which.

"Oh, yeah?" He scooted closer. We were friends now. "I heard it cost a pretty penny to go there." I shrugged. "So, tell me what you think of the members."

"Um, well, they're kind of intimidating. The girls my age all have perfect skin, hair, tans, nails. I don't really know how to keep up. That's why I'm here instead of at the pool."

"What do your parents think of you learning to drive trucks?"

"I think my mother really likes it. She's kinda proud of me. She thinks it's cool."

"What does she do?"

"She's an accountant."

"Well, she's a smart lady."

"Yeah, I like to think so. So, what do *you* think of the members?"

"You know, I gotta tell you." He laughed. "I gotta tell you, I get orders to split a damn hot dog. Split a damn hot dog! How you be a member of a country club and split a damn hot dog?"

I laughed. "Yeah. . . ."

"If I'm gonna be a member of a country club, I'm gonna *be* a member of a country club. I ain't splitting no damn hot dog."

I laughed because I knew what he meant; yet there are so many reasons to split a hot dog: to limit calories, to feed two little kids who won't eat a full one, or to save money.

"Y'all know you gotta wait like several years before working if you have a felony, right?" an instructor inter-rupted. *Where did that come from?*

"Hold on. I have to wait how long?" This came from the chef.

He was obviously joking. Right? What even quali-fied as a felony? Killing someone, probably. Opening mail addressed to someone else?

"Wait, but what if it's just a misdemeanor?" asked the man across from us. This conversation was *not* a joke.

"How many?"

"Like two or three."

"Oh, I wouldn't know about that."

I wasn't sure what the proper etiquette was after finding out someone was a felon. I wanted to know what had happened, but was I allowed to ask? Or was that rude? I didn't decide in time to question him because it was his turn to practice an offset.

Double Clutching

To practice changing gears, we went to the "shifting range," which was really just an abandoned parking lot. We practiced going back and forth without the trailer to make sure we had the basics of shifting down.

"Alright, Miss Abigail. You ready?" I nodded and got in the cab's passenger seat. "I'll show you first. It's just one, two. See? Clutch and take it out of gear, then clutch and put it in gear. Use the gas to make the RPM go up, see here? One, two. Easy. Now, your turn."

I nodded. I drove a manual. How different could it be? The instructor and I switched sides.

For starters, there were ten gears, not six. There was a high side and a low side, where gears one and six were paired, two and seven, three and eight, four and nine, and five and ten. Flipping a switch between five and six indicated a change from the low side to the high one. That would take some getting used to.

The gears grinded if I pressed the clutch too lightly or too hard. Or if I revved the engine too much or too little. I had to find the sweet spot. Downshifting entailed the same essentials, just with braking beforehand.

After a few weeks, I could practice in the shifting range consistently smoothly, so we went out on the road with the trailer. I loved sitting on the bed in the back of the cab, going along for the ride as other students drove. I couldn't wait to do it for real one day.

When my turn came, shifting and driving felt so natural.

"See how she's shifting those gears, and they're not grinding? See how she's not forcing it to go in? I want you to do the same." An instructor lectured the student in the back.

"Yeah, yeah. I see. She's pretty good."

"Yup, and you could be, too, if you just listened," the instructor reminded the guy. Then he turned to me and asked, "You're not a spy, are you?"

Recruiters

About once every couple of weeks at 7 Sons, recruiters from trucking companies would come visit to tell us about the advantages of signing with them: wages, bonuses, nice trucks, no-touch freight. As someone who couldn't do a full push-up, the last advantage spoke to me because it meant I could still drive without having to lift heavy products—I just had to back up and let someone else load the truck with freight.

Listening to the recruiters, my heart fluttered every time. I could see myself in a truck, my belongings traveling with me, no attachments back home, driving for hours upon hours, making good money. I could listen to music, eat whatever I wanted. That's all driving really was to me anyway.

Without fail, every presentation ended with the recruiter gazing at me and saying, "We are trying to be a diverse company. We have plenty of women truckers who would be able to help you, and we're looking to hire more women. You could also do team drives with the women, or husband-wife pairing."

"Oh, well, do you have local jobs?"

"No."

"Because I'm not twenty-one yet, so I can't cross state lines."

"You're not twenty-one?" At this point they'd laugh and continue with, "Forget it. Nobody's gonna hire you."

This is the point when the fire in my heart went out just a little bit. With each recruiter, I could see the reality behind their last statement. Nobody wanted me. These recruiters were just taking bodies, any and all of them, except mine.

The other students encouraged me, telling me I was unbelievably good and that I'll just have to wait, but all I felt was disappointment, again and again and again. Several times, I wondered what the point was. Why was I getting my CDL if nobody wanted me? But each time I realized that the only sure-fire way to not be hired as a truck driver was to not have a CDL. If I had a CDL, it didn't matter what companies said or whether I was hired because in the state of Virginia, I could drive a truck, and that would be enough for now.

Dermatologist

My mother's tennis friend from North Carolina came up to Richmond to visit us once. She took one look at my face and told me her unsolicited professional dermatologist opinion. I had acne scars, and I needed to take care of all the acne on my face before I could deal with the scars.

First of all, rude. Second of all, sold. My acne had stumped two Richmond dermatologists. I'd been through an entire year of isotretinoin, which is supposed to get rid of acne permanently after six to nine months. I'd tried all the typical topical ointments and oral medications, so I made an appointment and drove down to North Carolina. I would do whatever she told me to.

After she reviewed my history, she realized that I had severe acne since my face hadn't responded to anything. First, she would address my hormones, which hadn't been addressed before. She put me on birth control and spirono-lactone. My acne started disappearing but not enough for her. I was so glad to have someone like her on my side to point out my imperfections and tell me how to fix them.

After a few more visits, she wanted to put me back on isotretinoin. She theorized that my body hadn't absorbed the generic brand, so she'd put me on the name brand. I'd need two forms of birth control.

"Abstinence." That's what I'd used last time.

"Are you sure?"

"Yes." No boys in my foreseeable future.

"You can't change it halfway through."

"Okay." If I did get lucky enough to meet someone, I'd just have to tell them no. Easy.

CDL Training Certificate

The day before my CDL test, Malone came up to me and looked around before whispering, "You know, from what I've been hearing from the instructors, it sounds like we're sending our best student out tomorrow morning. You're gonna do great." I didn't believe him, and his confidence had made me even more nervous. Now I *had* to pass the next day. I didn't want to disappoint Malone and the other instructors. I wanted to prove them right.

No award or certificate of accomplishment had ever felt as gratifying as the one I received from 7 Sons CDL Training. The faint ink had been printed on the thinnest printer paper I'd ever touched, but Malone beamed with pride when he shook my hand in the privacy of his office and handed me the thin sheet. No presenter of an award had ever been so pleased. I, Abigail Olson, an eighteen-year-old girl, was his best student among all the rough, older men, and I had passed the DMV's CDL test on my first try. If I could do it without having any prior experience with trucks, anyone could do it with enough patience.

Malone handed me an "I did it!" t-shirt—extra-large, since that was the smallest size—that advertised 7 Sons. I

wore the shirt everywhere. Because I had done it. I priori-
tized passing this test over senior beach week and vacations
with friends. I sweated and cried for this. Some days weren't
ideal, but other days were great.

Malone took me outside for a picture in front of the
truck, my certificate in my hand. The photo went up on the
bulletin board that I'd studied during every lunch break. I
had dreamt of being up there. I had pictured my face among
the sea of people who didn't give up. It's not like anyone
would care about my picture posted in the office building,
but I cared. Now my picture is up there with others who
trained hours upon hours in a hot truck. I did it. I worked
for it. Nobody can take that away from me.

Cucumber Water

"Tina," I said to my best friend, "I want you to meet Gatlin."

"Why?"

"Because I like him! And I want you to like him, too."

She laughed. "You've been on *how* many dates with this guy again?"

"Like, two. Last night and this morning."

"Exactly."

"But I met his dad. That's supposed to be a big deal, right?"

"I'll meet him after you've been dating for a month."

"Like actually dating or just been going on dates for a month?"

"Actually dating."

"Ugh, okay." She was being so difficult. Like when she tells me to eat vegetables—cucumber water doesn't count.

First Kiss

While he was driving me home after two weeks of daily dates, Gatlin said, "So, the other day, I called you my girl-friend, and you didn't say anything. Does this mean . . . Do you want to be my girlfriend?"

"Sure! Let's do it! High-five!" I gave him a high-five.

"That's not what I was expecting."

"What were you expecting?"

"A kiss or something."

"You're driving. . . ."

For the rest of the ride, he rambled about how beautiful I was and how amazing I was. And perfect. And smart. And because I also had a fairly high opinion of myself, I ate up all of his compliments. And then we were at my front door.

"You haven't had your first kiss yet, have you?"

I laughed. It was about time for him to ask me. "Um, no, why?"

"Well, do you want to?"

"Um, sure."

"Sure?"

"I mean, yes. I do." I did. I remembered one of my friends told me kissing was like biting into a warm peach. I definitely wanted to know what that meant. And I felt comfortable with Gatlin. I felt ready. But I was nervous.

"Okay, so just lean in." I started laughing. I couldn't take him seriously. His face came at mine so fast. I jerked away. "What?"

"I'm so sorry. You look like a chicken."

"Your eyes aren't supposed to be open."

"But then how am I supposed to see you to match our lips?"

"What? No, it'll work. You'll see. Close your eyes."

I jerked away again. "I promise, I'll do it, I'll do it. Just hold on. I have to psych myself up for this."

"We can wait…"

"No, no. I want to. I promise. I'm just nervous."

"Okay, how about you kiss my cheek first."

"Okay. Yeah, I can do that." I kissed his cheek. *Easy.* And then his lips. *Done!* That wasn't so bad. Maybe I'd forgotten what peaches felt like, but that did not feel like a peach. Or terribly warm. I wasn't sure what I was expecting from a kiss, but the experience felt a bit anticlimactic. *I'll understand my friend's comment later. Hopefully.*

To Love is To Control (I)

"What would you have done if I said no when you asked me out?"

"I would've kept asking until you said yes. Even if you had a boyfriend."

—

"I still can't believe your dad got my number from searching y'all's phone records and then called me five times in the middle of the night."

"I know, I'm sorry. That was my fault. If I'd only answered him when he texted me, that wouldn't have happened."

"Gatlin, you don't control your dad's actions. That was his choice, not yours."

"I know. I still should've just answered him, though."

"Gatlin, if I hit you, and you hit me, did I make you hit me?"

"What? No!"

"It's the same thing. Everyone is responsible for their own actions."

"Yeah, but it still wouldn't have happened if I had texted him back."

—

"What would you do if I left you here?"

"I'd call an Uber. My phone's in my purse."

"That's why you always bring your purse? I thought it was just because you were one of those girls that always need chapstick."

"That, too."

"Why do you do that?"

"Why do you ask me what I'd do if you left me alone in a restaurant?"

"You're not allowed to bring your purse anymore."

"I'm bringing my purse."

—

"I still can't believe your dad's making us take pictures of the food before we put it in the cart. You know that's insane, right?"

"I know, I know, but that's just how he is."

"It looks like they're out of the meat he wants."

"He says they have it. He's never wrong. He's never made a mistake."

"He's never ever been wrong? Ever? Perfect one hundreds throughout school? Take a look at the shelves, Gatlin. Do you see the meat he's asking for?"

"He's online, and they have it in stock."

"I don't know what to say to that because I don't see it on the shelf."

"Here's someone. They're restocking the meat."

———

"So, how does working for your dad work? Does he pay you by the hour or output or salary?"

"Basically, if I do exactly what he says and wants, he pays for all of our dates."

"Doesn't he also plan all of our dates?"

"Not all of them."

———

"Last time I was here, everyone was liberal."

"How do you know?"

"None of the girls were wearing bras."

"What would you do if I didn't wear a bra?"

"You are *not* to go out in public without a bra on."

"You mean you would *like* for me to wear a bra in public?"

"I just don't want other guys thinking they have a chance with you."

"Don't you think that's determined by how I act, not what I wear?"

———

Bzz.

"Is that your dad?"

"Yeah. When I get home, he's making me eat."

"Why?"

"Because he says there's no way both of our lunches together was only fifteen dollars."

"How does he know how much it was? We just got back."

"He gets text notifications from the bank when I spend money."

Love

"I'd still love you."

That did *not* fit into our conversation. At all. We'd been hanging out at a Starbucks drinking hot chocolate. Wasn't that word supposed to be some big deal? In the movies, it is. They call it the "L-word." And, some of my friends had worried when their boyfriends hadn't said it yet. Should I have been grateful that I didn't have to deal with the stress of wondering whether or not he loved me?

"Okay."

"Did you hear me?"

"Yeah."

"I said that I love you."

"I know; I said I heard you."

"Well, do you love me?"

"We've been dating officially for two weeks. I feel like I'm still getting to know you. . . . I'm sorry. Are you mad?"

"I mean, it'd be nice if you said it back, but it's okay. I can wait. I love you, and I'll just wait until you love me, too."

"Okay, thanks. It'll probably be a while."

"I can wait."

He was happy for some reason. Giddy, almost. I couldn't tell why. He kind of seemed excited to wait for me to say I loved him.

The Constant Conversation

"I think we should do it."

"Okay."

"Is that a yes?"

"No?" I smiled at his audacity. "I was just acknowledging your desire."

"Oh." Gatlin and I kept kissing. "Please?"

"No." Was he serious?

"How about now?"

"No." I laughed. Nothing had changed in two seconds. What made him think something had?

"Please?"

"I can say no all day." I could. I'd been refusing every day for weeks and could continue doing so. I was glad I could use my dermatologist as an excuse to back up my decision, but I also wasn't ready. I thought it was cute that he believed asking me again and again would change my mind. That constantly begging would miraculously make me say yes.

I firmly believed that there was nothing he could say or do. The more he asked, the less comfortable I felt and the longer I wanted to wait. Besides, he couldn't force me to do anything I didn't want to.

Job Interview

"Have you ever driven a truck before besides taking the test?"

"No."

"Do you know how to fix a truck?"

"No."

"What about a car?"

"No. . . . I'm listening to myself talk, and I'm realizing I'm totally not qualified for this job."

"Well, yes, but all the applicants who do qualify are felons, so I have to choose."

—

I walked out of the interview and called my mother to say, "If I get the job, it's because I'm not a felon."

I applied to be a CDL driver and got an office job with minimal dump truck driving. I took anything I could get, especially after that interview, where I'd realized just how unqualified I was.

Making Out

Gatlin and I were making out on my couch when he pulled away. "I love you."

I smiled. "Okay." I leaned back in.

He pulled back. "I love you."

I smiled. "So you've said."

"Do you love me?"

I sighed. This was *not* the time for this conversation. If I said no, we'd have to stop kissing. But if I said yes, I'd have to mean it. Like *really* mean it. I'd been waiting for my heart to be so full of love that it'd be obvious to say that I love him, but technically speaking, would it be truthful to say I didn't love him? I loved all my friends and wasn't shy about letting them know. And we'd already established that Gatlin is more than a friend, so logically, I loved him, too. Right? Right.

"Um, yeah."

"You hesitated."

I sighed. Heavily. "I'm sorry. I love you."

"It's okay. I'm just glad you finally said it back."

To Love is To Control (II)

"I'm going to call you."

"You always happen to call me right when I'm on the toilet. It puts me in a weird situation because I see it, but should I answer?"

"Is that what happens? Not going to lie, every time you don't pick up, I get mad and think 'Oh, great, she's with another guy.' And then you call me two seconds later, and it's all good."

"Is that why you always sound so confrontational when I call back?"

—

"So, since you're busy tonight, Lola has invited me to go salsa dancing with her!"

"Okay."

"You okay?"

"I mean, I'm not going to stop you from going, but I'm not happy about the idea of you dancing with all those guys. I saw how they all looked at you."

First Lessons

My first day on the job, Bandit, the main CDL driver and one of the foremen, showed me the ropes: where to get scrap concrete, how to fill out the forms, which office building to go into, who to tell I was there and where I'd be.

I wanted to do so well. I heard my mother's voice reprimanding me when I failed to miss a pothole, so in the muddy scrap yard, I tried to avoid every single one, an almost impossible task.

"Why are you swerving? Those tires are made to go through all this."

"Oh, okay."

When we stopped in front of the office building to tell the receptionist we were here, I half-jogged to the door—it's important to be quick and efficient. I climbed back into the dump truck—three points of contact.

"Why are you running?"

"Oh, am I not supposed to do that?"

"You get paid by the hour, don't you? And, I'm gonna teach you to shift without using the clutch, or you'll tire your left leg out."

A Proposal

We were making out in his car about to get out to play mini golf. Anyone could have walked by and seen us. I was a bit uncomfortable with the public display of affection, but kissing him felt so good. I never wanted it to end, yet I was petrified someone I knew would look inside Gatlin's car.

"I forgot how good this feels," he said. He'd just gotten back from a week-long Thanksgiving trip.

"Do you want your gifts now?" I'd gotten him two books I thought he'd like.

He unwrapped them. "I love them!"

More kissing, of course.

"Okay, are you ready for yours?" He pulled away and reached into his coat pocket. "It's the most expensive gift I've gotten anyone for Christmas."

Since he'd Skyped me the day he bought my gift, I already knew what it was: an emerald and gold ring. He'd known that green was my favorite color and that I preferred gold-colored jewelry over silver. How romantic. I took the ring, but we started making out again before I could put it on.

"Let's just make this official," Gatlin said, taking the ring from my hand. "Abigail, will you—?"

"Stop, stop, stop! It's too soon."

Obviously, I wasn't dating Gatlin thinking we'd break up, but logically speaking, one month is too soon to know someone enough to make that serious of a call. I could tell in his eyes that he meant it. He really loved me. He actually wanted to marry me. We'd talked about it before, but I'd thought of our chats as theoretical and optimistic about the future. I hadn't realized he was serious.

But can you marry someone who genuinely believes you're perfect? What do you do when it's too soon, but you have no specific objections to it? How can you stop your brain from jumping to that frame of mind? What happened to the slow courtship of just being with someone without having to decide?

How could I not want to marry someone so pure, so eager? Someone so strong, so good looking? But why the rush? Couldn't we just live in moments of handholding and snuggles for a little longer? And what did marriage mean to Gatlin? To me?

In that moment, we made a secret pact. We would plan to get married someday, but we'd wait a little longer to announce an official engagement. From that point on, Gatlin called me his fiancée, if the small technicality could be omitted. He sent messages about husbands and wives. He pointed out houses for future children. He dreamt of me at home supporting him and of him providing material goods for his kids. All this a month in.

It felt like elementary school all over again, except this time it was real. Real ring, real intentions, real adults. Do people really grow up? Had we grown up as much as we thought? Were we just playing house, or did we have the kind of love that would last a lifetime?

Preparing for an Interview

Gatlin was over a couple hours late. No text. No call. Was he even planning on showing up? I locked the door, turned off the lights, and went up to my bed. I would just watch a movie and cry myself to sleep. I didn't need him anyway. But fifteen minutes into the movie, the doorbell rang, and I was ready to give him a hard time.

I opened the door, and my hardened heart softened upon seeing Gatlin's face. Holding the phone slightly away from his ear, he mouthed, "It's been like this all day."

I could hear his dad berating him on the phone. "You need to listen, Gatlin. I told you to prepare for your coding job interview tomorrow, and you didn't hear me, so get a piece of paper and write these down. You need to prepare."

I ran to get a pad of paper and a pen, while Gatlin went to sit on the couch.

"Do you have a piece of paper? Do you have it? Okay, these are the questions they're going to ask you. Why are you in Richmond? Are you prepared to answer that? Because they *will* ask you this. How did you start as a junior developer? Why are you leaving? Where are you from? Can you answer these questions? Are you writing these down? You need to practice. I see here you have 'wrestling'? And what is this exercise stuff you're doing in the morning? Can you tell me about that? Are you a Redskins fan? Gatlin, they're going to ask you these questions, and you're not going to be able to answer them unless you practice like I've said. Are you a Trump supporter? Black lives matter? How do you feel about abortion? Or working with a gay person? How do you feel about your wife working? They *will* ask you these questions, and you need to be able to answer. Are you going to practice?"

Gatlin's dad threw out the questions faster than we could write them down. And then I started to wonder. Why did Gatlin need to *practice* answering why he was in Richmond and where he grew up? What was there to practice? Weren't those pretty straightforward answers? Was that why all of his answers to my seemingly simple questions sounded rehearsed? He'd told me he'd moved to Richmond for job opportunities, but now he was applying all over the country because he still worked for his dad.

Things never really lined up with Gatlin. Why would he move halfway across the country to work for his dad when his dad flew back home every week? And Gatlin was originally supposed to move to Richmond on his own. What was going on over there? Was Gatlin just not very smart, or was something else happening? Either way, he didn't seem very happy.

When we hung up an hour later, I turned to Gatlin. "I'm so sorry you have to go through that."

"It's always like that. I just usually hide it."

That night, Gatlin looked so innocent, so pure, so beaten down. He looked like a little boy, not sure where to go or what to do. In that moment, my heart opened and let him in. I just wanted to take care of him, to make it all go away. I wanted him to feel safe with me and to know I would help him in any way he needed. In that moment, I decided to be more patient when he got angry, to be more understanding. He was going through a tough time. He used to get mad when I hesitated to say, "I love you, too," and at how the words never really came out smoothly. I resolved to say it back, and quickly, to verbally reassure him.

Lock the Doors, Shut the Blinds

"If Naomi from B2 calls, tell her Roger's not here. She's looking for money."

As a receptionist, my main duty was gatekeeping. I liked being in on the drama, but who was I to stand in the way of all these companies getting their money? Didn't they have the legal right to be compensated for their services? And if our company didn't have the resources to pay for these products and services, then why did Roger's Construction purchase them in the first place? Why couldn't we communicate that we were trying to obtain more cash?

The questions remained unanswered. My job was to turn people away and put on a friendly face. When I reported a call from someone saying Roger's Construction had to pay by a certain date, my superior's response was, "Or what?" Technically, she was right. What were these people going to do? Sue over four hundred dollars? Roger's Construction's bank account had "negative dollars," according to Lucy, the bookkeeper, so it's not like they would've gotten paid. But where was Roger's desire to maintain healthy business relationships with communication, civility, and payments?

Brring.

"Hi, thank you for calling Roger's Construction. This is Abigail. How may I help you?"

"Hi, Abigail. Is Roger there?"

"Yes! Hold on just one second. Who may I say is calling?"

"Naomi."

Oops, I'd totally forgotten. I was told she'd call three hours prior, so when she didn't, I'd written her off. She sounded so friendly! I hadn't been expecting such an amicable voice. What was I supposed to do now?

"Oh, okay, hold on." I put Naomi on hold and walked down the hall.

Knock. Knock. I knocked on Roger's open office door.

"Naomi's on the phone. I accidentally told her you were here."

"Tell her I'm on a long phone call."

As I walked back to my desk, I chastised myself. I couldn't believe I had messed this up. I had one job. I do nothing all day but sit at the desk twirling my thumbs, and they'd asked only this one thing of me.

"Hi, Naomi? He's on the phone right now, but I can take a message."

"It's okay. I can stay on the line. I'm not doing anything else."

"I think it's going to be a long call." I was not good at lying.

"That's okay. It's about accounts payable."

If I'd learned about anything during my time at Roger's Construction, it was accounts payable. That department pays invoices, and if they don't, every phone call is for them. Except Naomi didn't want accounts payable. She wanted the boss.

"Naomi says she's going to wait."

"Just tell her I'm not here."

How in the world was I supposed to go from him being in the office on a call to him being gone? I had totally dug myself into this mess, and I had no idea how to get out. I formulated a wonderful plan: just hang up.

Brring.

"Hi, thank you for calling Roger's Construction. This is Abigail. How may I help you?"

"Hi, Abigail. This is Naomi again. I think we got disconnected."

I immediately realized the folly in my unbelievably idiotic plan. Naomi even had the grace to blame it on a poor connection.

"Oh, hi, Naomi! I'm so sorry about that. Roger . . . left."

"He knew I was on the phone and then left?"

". . . Yes?"

"How unprofessional. He never responds to my emails, his voicemail is full, and he's never there when I call. I mean, does that sound professional to you? Maybe you can tell me how I may better reach him? What else should I try, Abigail?"

Naomi was so friendly and exasperated. I'd never want to be in her position. I wanted to help her but didn't know how.

"I'm not sure."

"You know what? I can be there in five minutes. I'll be there in five minutes."

"Okay! See you soon!"

Honestly, I was relieved. I could see how Roger would handle the situation. Maybe I could learn from him. I went to tell him.

"Naomi said she'd be here in five minutes."

"I don't have time for this." Roger grabbed his lunch and said, "Lock the doors, shut the blinds." With that, he left.

Lucy showed me exactly what to do. How did we have a procedure for avoiding independent contractors trying to collect their money but not for paying invoices?

A Dream

They took me onto a boathouse. You were somewhere. I couldn't see you, but I knew they took you, too. They had me in the kitchen, and I had this feeling that you were just outside the door—on the deck or something. One of them went to go check on you, and the kinda cute one stayed behind to make sure I didn't leave.

I sorta flirted with him. I know I shouldn't have. I'm really sorry, but I couldn't really help myself. It was just a dream, anyway. It didn't mean anything. I promise.

Then we kissed, and you weren't anywhere. I didn't think you'd come back, so I kissed him. He was kinda cute. Not all the way cute, just kinda.

Anyway, then things got way out of control. When you were gone, he took me to the sofa. We kept making out, but then I remembered you and how much I loved you and how what I was doing was wrong.

I started feeling guilty and all, so I tried to stop him, but he didn't listen. I tried pushing him off, but he was too strong. I called for you, but I guess the other guy stopped you from coming in. Or maybe you just couldn't hear me.

I'm so sorry. It doesn't mean anything. It was just a dream. I promise. I don't even know them in real life, so it's not like I was fantasizing about anyone or anything, but I am really sorry.

Then you told me that it was okay. Not "okay" in the way that you understood or in the way that it really was okay, but in the way that that's what you were supposed to say. And you said that if anything like that happened in real life, you'd be there for me. And I felt safe. You said you'd punch any guy who did that to me, and after everything, I believed you, not even realizing you'd already done that to me, not even realizing my dream had been about you.

Tax Evasion and Payroll

"Hey, Luiz, it's Abigail."

"Abi! Hey!"

"Do you know where Chava is?"

"Yeah, he's back there."

"Back where? In the yard behind the office?"

"No. Behind me."

"Oh . . . well, where are you?"

"Driving back from Fredericksburg."

"Okay, well, can you tell him to come to the office when y'all get back?"

I'd been tasked to discreetly find out everyone's pant and shirt sizes. For Christmas, the company was going to give all the workers hundred-dollar jackets or bibs, depending on whether they'd received a jacket for a previous Christmas. Additionally, every employee would get a ham and a $100 Visa gift card.

While I didn't want to complain, I was definitely confused. I'd answered all the threatening phone calls and handled all the visits, and I was the one who opened all the final notices that came in the mail. Running errands, I saw the merchants decline Roger's Construction's cards, and I made excuses on behalf of the machine when I knew the real problem. Yet here Roger's Construction was sending me off to purchase matching Carhartt jackets and bibs to be embroidered in time for the holidays.

I'm sure my bosses' intents were pure, to give freely for Christmas, but when I arrived home with all my booty, my mother, an accountant, claimed it was technically tax evasion. Any gift from employer to employee worth over twenty dollars should be flowed through payroll or reported to the IRS as income. She said, "Bonuses technically flow through payroll, so in the past, bosses would give their employees expensive gifts, such as fancy cars. Then they could say 'Oh, it's a gift' and not have to pay taxes on it. So, the government said that if companies wanted to do a nice gesture on Christmas, then they could do up to twenty dollars. Or twenty-five, I can't remember the exact details." On a much smaller scale, that's exactly what Roger's Construction did. But then, my mother recommended that I claim the ham on my tax return.

"What am I supposed to do? Mail the IRS twenty-five percent of a cooked ham?"

"No," my mom explained, annoyed at my sass. She knew I knew the answer and was just trying to be difficult. "Your tax rate times the monetary value of the ham."

As a receptionist/dump truck driver making thirteen

dollars an hour and paying my mother five hundred a month in rent along with trying to cover all my own costs, including acne medicine, I was not keen on the concept of giving the government money when I hadn't even received money. If they wanted to be paid a share of my ham, they could take some of the frozen soup in my freezer. They'll get as much use out of it as I did.

Although, to be fair, I must admit that the ham saved me quite a number of meals. I therefore probably could've afforded the extra cash to pay taxes on it.

I decided that the ham was probably around twenty dollars, so I didn't report that, but I reported the gift card when I sold it to my mother for ninety-five dollars, five dollars being the cost of cash's convenience. Profits from a business aren't taxed the same as wages, but I wasn't sure how else to report the income easily.

When I got back to work after Christmas, Roger's Construction received a final notice from Dominion Energy. I apprised our bookkeeper that they would cut off the power in three weeks if we didn't pay three bills.

"Okay." She shrugged.

"'Okay' as in we're going to pay them or 'okay' as in we won't have lights in three weeks?"

"The second."

That Thursday, I overheard the bookkeeper talking to

our bosses, a husband and wife couple, while they were still on vacation in West Virginia.

"Tomorrow's gonna be a shit show with payroll. . . . I have three dollars on my desk, and there's no money in the accounts. . . ."

I looked up what happens when a company files for bankruptcy. Would the employees get paid for their time? The order of payment to people owed money goes to secured loans then unsecured loans. It made sense, but I wasn't sure whether employees would be qualified as either, given the fact that we didn't loan any money—just time. To this day, I'm still not sure of that fact, but I am definitely sure that if I ever give a loan, it will be secured with some kind of collateral.

I went to bed that night excited for the next day. Of course, I wanted my paycheck, but I'd sacrifice it for two reasons: watching a "shit show" and learning how a business failed (and if Roger's Construction didn't fail, how employees would handle not getting paid).

Fortunately for Roger's Construction, and unfortunately for my curiosity, a check for snow removal came in two hours before employees were supposed to get paid. It was just enough to cover payroll. The "accountant" received an angry lecture from Roger when they got back from West Virginia. She quit the next day. They blamed everything on her poor bookkeeping skills, yet a month later when the internet didn't work, my boss's immediate assumption came from another threatening notice and he concluded the internet got shut off—as opposed to simply checking the router.

Yes

No to this. No to that. I feel like a broken record. When was the last time I said yes? No has become an automatic response rather than a thoughtful answer. I say no so quickly these days. No to a formal engagement. No to sex. And what did those no's get me? A bunch of I don't knows.

I don't know if he still sees a forever future with me. I don't know if I should wear that ring on my middle finger anymore, especially since its edges dig into my skin. If my life were a book, an English teacher would go crazy over the symbolism. Wait, what? Why am I thinking that way? I'm in a relationship. And, I'm happy. Obviously. Otherwise, I'd end it. Of course.

And most importantly, I don't know what happened one night a few weeks ago. I know he doesn't talk about it, but he struts around like he remembers. I know that saying no didn't help then, that saying no now won't change the past.

But what if I say yes? Maybe that'll retroactively change the past. If I say yes now, maybe that means I also meant yes that night. And I won't have to be confused anymore. And if I say yes, I can regain control over my body.

To Love is To Control (III)

"Hey, so my parents want to make sure that you know we'll be spending every holiday with them when we get married."

"My mother and I don't celebrate holidays for a reason. Also, this is not the time to ask me that. I haven't even met your mom and your parents are already trying to force me to do something? Now, if we're together, and spur of the moment you want to make Christmas cookies or something, yeah, I'm totally down. But right now, there's no formal invitation to accept or decline."

"I know. They just want us to promise we will."

"Gatlin, there's too much pressure attached, and you didn't even seem happy when you went! I'm not agreeing to that. When we're married, they can invite us, and we can accept or decline, and you can go without me. I'm not forcing you to stay back."

"No. Just say yes."

"We're not even engaged! I still haven't met half your family!"

"Just say yes now, and we can say no later. We just have to make them happy."

"Tell them whatever you want to, but I'm not lying."

—

"Oh, I wonder why Jimmy is texting me."

"What's he saying?"

"He wants to ask a favor."

"A favor? You must've been talking to him for a while then."

"No. This is completely out of the blue."

"It's weird to just ask someone for a favor."

"He says he wants me to drive him to Maryland to pick out a motorcycle, and he'd compensate me for my efforts."

"He doesn't have anyone else he can ask?"

"Probably, but we'd talked about it a couple months before you and I started dating, and he knows I like driving."

"That's not something you just say to someone randomly. Are you sure you weren't talking to him before?"

"Yes. Remember when we were at the movie theater, and a girl texted you 'Hey' and you wanted to make sure I knew y'all weren't talking? And I said it was okay and I understand things like that happen randomly? This is the same thing, except Jimmy and I are actually friends. We were buds in ninth grade biology and twelfth grade military history."

"All my past girlfriends claimed they were 'just friends' until they cheated on me. So, what're you going to say to him?"

"I'm not sure yet."

"Up to you. Just know that if you go, we're done."

—

"I don't understand why you're upset. I had lunch with my sister because she just got home, and then we had dinner as a family to make a plan for my life."

"We'd made plans for Friday night to celebrate my birthday and to eat out and then watch a movie. That morning, you told me you decided to work a shift that night instead. I started crying, which I admit is a bit unreasonable, but then you said, 'I'll see you Monday, no matter the weather, and if not, then for sure for sure Tuesday for lunch.' Well, today is Wednesday, and you actively signed up, without prompting, to work another shift Monday, and then Tuesday, you didn't come by for lunch and skipped MMA, a sacred event I never come above, to plan with your dad, something you can do any time of any day. And the worst part is, you never told me. I waited all day yesterday for a text from you to tell me you couldn't make it. I didn't eat lunch, just in case. Like an idiot, I kept hoping you'd come, even after I saw your sister's Instagram story of y'all at lunch together."

"I just can't make you happy. I'm busy, and you know it. I was tired Monday, and Tuesday, I hadn't seen my sister in days. Nothing I do makes you happy."

—

"The necklace was super expensive. Hopefully that makes up for . . . everything."

Driving the Volvo

Peace feels like wind blowing through open windows. Freedom is cranking up the faltering radio system. Acceptance comes with receiving the common two-finger acknowledgement from passing truck drivers. Ignorance reveals itself by returning the slight movement with an emphatic five-finger wave.

After the other drivers reacted to my enthusiastic smile with a quizzical look, I became conscious of my small, five-foot-eight body bouncing in the seat. I could tell I didn't quite belong, except for the fact that I did. I belonged because I drove a dump truck. I belonged because I'd passed the same test they did. They didn't care that I was a girl. They knew I had as much of a right as they did to deliver scrap concrete and asphalt. They only questioned why I was so excited.

I was excited because CDL drivers don't acknowledge normal vehicles, only ones that require skill, and they acknowledged me. I was excited because I'd been accepted into the untouchable and ubiquitous community. Driving the Volvo was the closest to peace and freedom I'd felt in a while: the wind in my hair; the unavoidable potholes; the rocking of the vehicle when Pete, who worked at Roger's concrete distributor, loaded the bed; the tangible productivity I contributed to society; the calm, slow environment.

When I was in that truck, I didn't want to be anywhere else. I didn't want to think about anything except where I was headed. I lived completely in the moment, enjoying the fresh air. This is what I was meant to do. I picked up concrete half a mile down the road and dumped the scraps in the yard behind the office. Back and forth, back and forth. I could've sat there all day every day. I couldn't go any farther because the company's insurance policy didn't cover me as a driver under twenty-one.

As the morning passed, all I could think was, *I hope I don't get called back into the office. I hope I don't get called back. I hope they won't need me.* But, of course, by then, Jackie and Roger had figured out that I was "a machine" at office work and needed me to do various tasks, so I had only been able to do a couple rounds of picking up and dumping concrete.

Maybe if driving was my only job, I'd enjoy every minute of the day, but instead my job was to answer phones and copy business card information into an Excel spreadsheet and watch the business flounder, which certainly wasn't enough to fill nine hours each day.

To Love is To Control (IV)

"Our kids *will* be doing their homework."

"Gatlin, we don't even have kids. We're not even engaged! But I think we can come at it with a gentler approach than that harshness."

"Right, okay, I need to work on my communication skills. How do you feel about spanking? This is really important."

"I honestly haven't given it much thought."

"Oh, and my kids *will* be wrestlers and play football. They have to."

"They don't *have* to do anything."

—

"You know it's pointless for me to wear a condom, right? Because probabilities aren't additive. We're just relying on your birth control because birth control works ninety percent of the time and condoms only work eighty percent of the time."

"You're right. Probabilities aren't additive. I haven't researched the effectiveness of types of birth control, but assuming your numbers are correct, the condom doesn't work twenty percent of the time. Of that twenty percent, my birth control will be effective ninety percent of the time, meaning that instead of a ten or twenty percent chance of me getting pregnant, it's now only ten percent *of* twenty percent. Besides, you're lucky we're even having sex when I'm on this medicine that causes birth defects, and I told my dermatologist that abstinence would be my form of birth control."

—

"I keep thinking about you and Ken."

"What about it?"

"It's just . . . I feel like there's more to it than what either of you are telling me."

"What do you mean? Did he tell you something more?"

"No, we haven't talked since you told me about him."

"I don't know what else to say. We matched on Tinder a few months before I knew you existed, he said 'Teach me how to dance!' because dancing was in my bio, so I suggested salsa that Friday, we exchanged a few more texts, then a couple hours before we were supposed to go, he told me he couldn't because his mom's boyfriend's son was flying in from Ohio—"

"That was a lie."

"What?"

"That was a lie. His mother hasn't had a boyfriend in two years."

"Oh, I didn't know that. He obviously played me."

"He's had an on-and-off girlfriend for two years."

"Okay? So it must've been one of the off times."

"I don't know. . . . It still doesn't make sense. There must be something more. When I told him I liked you, he acted like he'd never heard of you."

"He probably forgot. I must not have been a memorable encounter."

"But then he never came back to the early morning workouts, even though he'd paid for a full year and promised me he'd go every day."

"I don't know what to say. I feel like you gotta ask him about that one."

"And he knew we were dating because he said, 'How are you and your girlfriend?' I just feel like there's something more between you two."

"It was probably a joke, or he could tell? I don't know how he knew if you didn't tell him."

"There's something more."

"I told you everything when I found out a few months ago that Ken was your best friend here in Richmond. I thought it was funny that your best friend and girlfriend matched on Tinder, and nothing happened way before either of us knew you. Besides, I deleted my account. I don't even have his number."

"I know. I just don't understand."

—

"It just feels like I'm your last priority even though you tell me I'm your first."

"Abigail, do you know what healthcare and coding are?"

"What're you talking about?"

"They're round-the-clock jobs. How much do you think married couples even see each other?"

"All the fucking time because they're fucking married?"

"Hey. You will *not* speak to me that way. I'm going to want to coach my kids' sports teams—that's evenings and weekends."

"Which is it? Last week, you were talking about going into the military and being gone for eight years. You can't do both. Also, you keep saying that when we're married, you want to have sex a lot. I'm cool with that, but that's not all I want us to be, and it's increasingly sounding like that's all you want to allow time for."

Why I'm Staying

I'm staying because I have a weakness for nice arms. He's strong. And fast. And cute.

I'm staying because he and his friends and I are supposed to go fishing sometime. He and I are supposed to do a Spartan race together in a few months. We have so many fun outdoorsy activities to do in our future.

I'm staying because I love waiting for the doorbell to ring, for the promise of a romantic evening. Because everything bad that happened before is just an exception, not how our relationship actually is.

I'm staying because of the way he puts his arms around me. The way his little touches assure me everything is going to be okay. We are okay.

I'm staying because I can fix this. I can make everything better, if only he'll listen to me instead of his dad. I can convince him.

I'm staying because who else is there?

I'm staying because no one else sees through him. Because I don't want to admit that I'm crazy. For falling for him in the first place. For not thinking he's great when his friends worship him. For putting in so much effort that will all be for nothing if I leave.

I'm staying because he loves me. And I've verbally committed myself to him. Because I shouldn't leave someone I love. Ever. That's what it means to love someone. Right?

Why Every Woman Needs Her CDL

"You're not dressed to be out here," called a man as I walked to the yard behind Roger's Construction.

It was one of those rainy sixty-five-degree January days that Virginia can sometimes have, so I'd worn a skirt and flip flops for the warmer weather. I'd given up on wearing the appropriate attire for driving since I never knew when I'd be asked to drive and weeks would go by without driving. Flip flops especially were a driving no-no; they could limit control of a vehicle if it was manual. Some workers got to know me as the dump truck driver girl who wore flip flops. I really would've preferred not to wear unsafe attire, but to wear muddy shoes in an office environment would've been inappropriate and messy. My gold Jack Rogers felt more office appropriate.

The yard contained heavy equipment, a dump truck, and sundry materials for delivery. The man who'd called out to me wasn't an employee of Roger Construction, so I assumed he was working on the many machines that needed fixing.

Looking down at my cute skirt and flip flops sinking into the muddy ground, I smiled and said, "Yeah, I didn't know I'd be out here today."

I kept walking to the Volvo dump truck and climbed in. As I turned the ignition and started driving away, I looked down at the man, who couldn't take his eyes off me as he watched me leave. I could tell he was embarrassed. He'd just poked fun at an unassuming young girl who could do something he most likely couldn't. He'd talked down to her like she didn't fit in, but he didn't know what she was capable of.

I found early on that driving a dump truck was the quickest way to earn respect. Nobody dared mess with someone who could do that. I wasn't sure why. Maybe it was due to the patience it took or the fact that I could run them over. Whatever the reason, there was awe and power in having that ability. It was the kind of protection and confidence that helped women who've grown up catcalled.

This is why I wanted to get my CDL. I didn't have to say a single thing. He not only backed off, but he gave me respect. Instantaneously.

This happened when I went to the DMV for my driving record: "Oh, no. Something's off. Wait, you have your CDL at eighteen? Don't see that every day. . . ." And again, when I went to get a drug screening for a job: "This isn't right. You're here for a DOT drug test? Wow."

Immediate respect. My actions spoke for themselves over and over. They communicated that I was a woman who could take care of herself. No matter where I went or what I did, the confidence went with me, and the power shone through.

Driving the Kenworth

"Hello?"

"Hey, I heard you're about to drive the Kenworth, and I'm calling to let you know that it shuts off. When it does that, take it out of gear, turn the truck off, then back on, then press the engine start button, and then put it back into gear. When you're doing all that, the power steering won't be working, so, yeah, just be careful."

Charlie was the official CDL driver for Roger's Construction, but on days when there were too many deliveries, I'd pitch in. Because I wasn't on the company's insurance policy, the day's trip would be short, but on the other hand, I didn't know where I was going. I thought Roger had told me to take a right, but I couldn't find where I was supposed to dump, so I looked up the directions on my phone, which told me to turn around—I should've taken a left. Apparently, Google hadn't updated when the customer had moved offices. After I had taken quite a while longer than expected, the customer called to give me directions. I *was* supposed to have taken a right turn.

Charlie had been right; the truck kept cutting off every couple of minutes. When I got back to the office, I told

Jackie, my supervisor and Roger's wife, about the faulty vehicle. Two weeks later, she told me the Kenworth was fixed and asked me to go pick up a few loads of concrete. The truck ran smoothly until Pete started dumping scraps of concrete into the bed. After the second time it shut off, I kept it off until I had to return to the office. On my way back to the yard, the time between each shut off decreased until the truck wouldn't start back up again. I started rolling backwards down the hill and had to put on the emergency air brakes.

That's when I started getting worried. What if a car had been right behind me? I realized I wasn't in complete control of the dangerous equipment and could cause harm, from which I had no financial protection.

I called Jackie. I called Lucy. Then Alex, the mechanic. I called Bandit, another of Roger's Construction's CDL drivers. I called Jackie again. Alex. Bandit. Nobody picked up. I called Charlie, but he couldn't help because he was far away on a different run. The truck's battery was running low. The low air pressure warning system started beeping. Alex called back to say it'd been working fine for twenty minutes the night before and to tell me to just try again. I did, and it worked. It was possible that the truck just worked for twenty minutes at a time.

When I got back to the office, I told Jackie I wasn't

driving that truck again. If other people wanted to drive the truck and risk their safety, that was fine, but I wasn't willing to sacrifice it just to pick up a load of concrete. Jackie agreed.

A few weeks later, Charlie went on his honeymoon, and I dropped off the Volvo for a fog light recall, a short in the brake circuit, a hydraulic leak, and a couple other maintenance issues. The Volvo was the "working" dump truck.

The day Charlie got back, he took the Kenworth to haul a few dirt loads for Adam, with whom Roger had worked out a bartering system. When the Kenworth broke down in an intersection, Adam pretended to be a Roger's Construction employee to pick up the Volvo from the dealership before it was fixed. Charlie continued to haul dirt until he realized the brake light was not only not working, but the entire wiring system had been taken out. A DOT ticket for that could hinder his ability to find another job, not to mention it was illegal and unsafe.

Roger and Adam attempted to pressure Charlie into continuing to drive the Volvo, and Jackie told him to bring the Kenworth back to the office. Charlie did the latter only because I tailed him to make sure I could be there if something went wrong again. When we got back to the office, Roger gave Charlie hell for not just fixing the light himself. The conversation, littered with curse words, is not worth repeating, but Charlie later told me, "I don't know what to say. There are wires sticking out where they're not supposed to be. I'm not an electrician."

I realized then that, although Charlie's job description was my end goal, I did not want to be in his shoes. He was not only expected to drive the trucks but be the mechanic for them because Roger would rather spend three days discussing the issue than pay a hundred and fifty dollars to have a professional fix it in an hour. The DMV didn't test potential professional drivers on electrical and mechanical problems, only the parts to know what they should look like in case something goes wrong. While they are adjacent jobs, electrician and mechanic careers are not the same as a driving one. I wouldn't have minded learning how to fix a short in a circuit (it's just physics, right?) or how to fix a dump truck, but I wouldn't have wanted to be expected to know it without any formal or informal education.

I quit the next week. I hadn't applied to be the receptionist, and I realized I didn't want to be a driver for Roger's Construction, as free as I felt in the trucks and as much as I felt in my soul that driving them was my passion.

Virginia Beach

An entire day at the beach, just the two of us. It had sounded so charming, but the romanticism of what could've been stopped me from realizing how it really was. Gatlin loved Virginia Beach, and he couldn't wait to share his special places with me. For many weeks, I'd heard tales of him, his dad, and his sister spending two months there, bouncing from hotel to hotel, wherever was cheapest for the night. His dad was smart like that.

We first stopped at Gatlin's favorite breakfast place. The waitresses recognized him and struck up an energetic conversation in the manner of long-lost best friends. It felt like a ploy to remind himself and me that every girl wished she could be in my place and I was lucky to be dating a guy so personable. I was crazy for crying so much after our interactions when everyone lit up when they saw him.

Gatlin recommended the sweet potato pancakes. After I told him I didn't like sweet potatoes, he ordered the pancakes himself. When they arrived, he cut a bite and brought the fork to my tight-lipped mouth, at one point trying to pry open my lips and jaw with the other hand.

"Try it."

"No, thanks."

"You don't love me if you don't try it."

"My love for you is not tied to my eating certain foods. Besides, no means no," I reminded him.

And that's when he said it: something so incredibly unbelievable, something that admitted the sin he'd committed a month before. "That's not what it meant when you said it about sex." Not only had he verbalized it without guilt, but he'd tried to *persuade* me with these words.

I looked at the grin on his face, like he'd finally just won an argument with me. Did he know what he'd just said? Did he mean it the way it sounded? Or was he just throwing back in my face the time I finally said yes to his incessant begging because I knew how much it'd make his night? Did that night invalidate all future times I'd say no? Or was it the night I trusted him and didn't fight back that made him say this? Did he think he could just overpower me physically and get his way? That I'd give in and wouldn't put up a fight?

I'd had enough. My heart hardened. I envisioned myself walking right out the door, leaving him behind to chase me, to beg for mercy, but when I stood up, his hand gripped my wrist. I pulled, and he tightened. I couldn't leave the table. Wondering if she'd noticed, I looked at the waitress. She was watching a game on TV, completely oblivious. There was no way I could overcome Gatlin, and even if I could leave him behind in my angry dust, where would I go? He'd driven me two hours from Richmond.

I couldn't get home, so I stayed. I tried the sweet potato pancake, and it left a bad taste in my mouth. The waitress approached to take away our plates.

"Did you try the sweet potato pancake?" she asked me.

"Yeah, I got her to try it," Gatlin replied with his charismatic smile.

"It's good, isn't it?"

"The best," he answered for me.

Gatlin left a fifty percent tip before we left for our next adventure. He'd brought his football to play catch, but I suddenly had a headache. Probably from dehydration or something. I wanted so badly to be the smiling girl in cute shorts, passing a football to her strong boyfriend on the beach. There really isn't anything more picturesque. I had the beach, the strong boyfriend, the football, the cute shorts. I just couldn't muster the smile, the only thing missing. Damn that headache preventing the final touch to this movie scene. Damn my oncoming stomachache. How was I supposed to enjoy this romantic day with all my physical ailments?

We spent the day walking along the beach. He showed off how he could climb up a rope without using his feet. I bought Advil at a CVS. By the end of the trip, his watch had recorded around eleven miles of walking.

Later that evening, we ordered a pizza and drove back to my house, eating in the car. Nothing settles me like a nice, long drive. I cranked up the country music and focused on being in the moment. Nothing mattered besides watching the trees slip away and losing myself in the songs. I left that day behind.

When Gatlin pulled into the driveway, his hands were already down my pants. I missed kissing. I missed nonsexual touching. I missed everything that led up to the moment he keeps jumping to, the touches that made it that much more special and intimate. It's not like we ever had time for both intimacy and sex, so of course, he'd always opt for the latter. That night, we only had fifteen minutes before he had to leave to drive back to his apartment. His dad had ordered him to be home by eight thirty.

Four minutes passed, and I finished. Three more and so did he. I was glad it was over, not because I didn't enjoy the act, but because the time pressure stressed me out. I felt rushed, animalistic. He'd stop if I said something hurt—he wouldn't dare cross *that* line—but he was always too into his own body and mind to hear what I was really saying.

"I'm not very comfortable."

Gatlin grinned and pulled out a second condom. "Think we can do it again?"

"No. I'm tired, and it's almost time for you to go."

"Let's do it."

With eight minutes left and not another word, he started again. His phone buzzed. For once, his dad's constant badgering didn't distract him. I tried flexing and unflexing my muscles down there, hoping I could be strong enough to physically push him out, since he stopped listening to my words long ago.

At the end of those eight minutes, Gatlin said, "I can tell when you're not as into it. You're drier and tighter." He made it sound like an achievement that he knew me and my body so well.

That was the night he said, "Yeah, I'm never leaving." More to himself than to me.

Part of me rejoiced at those words, and the other part of me wondered what I had done to make him want to leave me. Because the thought of leaving me had to have crossed his mind for him to confirm he wouldn't.

Green Beans

A strainer full of green beans sat beside me in the passenger seat. My mother had handed them to me through the car window when I stopped in the driveway for two seconds after work before heading to get my eyebrows threaded.

I sat in a parking lot, talking to Gatlin on the phone. I looked at the clock, waiting until my appointment, maximizing my time with Gatlin. As long as we talked, I had hope that everything would be okay. I had hope that I could fix whatever was bothering him or whatever was eating at me.

6:30 pm. The last thing I ate was lunch the afternoon before. That lunch had been a little nibble of a sandwich. I hadn't been hungry then, and I wasn't hungry talking to Gatlin.

I wanted to eat those green beans. My mother told me to. I knew I should've been hungry, but the thought of eating made me want to throw up. Maybe I just wanted to throw up because they were green beans and I didn't like vegetables. What if I'd had a pizza beside me? No. I wouldn't have eaten that either. Cheeseburger with fries and a root beer? No. Ice cream? No. Maybe something light like a milkshake? No. What was wrong with me? I could stomach a few sips from my water bottle. Yes, I'd drink some water.

"Okay, I have to go. Bye, love you."

As I walked to Chaha's, I noticed my slim reflection in the windows. I looked great! I wondered if my loose skinny jeans had anything to do with my appetite . . . maybe. But it wasn't like I'd been *trying* to lose weight. I just wasn't hungry.

Meetings

"Abigail, go to an Al-Anon meeting, and then we can talk."

I'd been crying all morning, draining my mother's energy during tax season of all times. But a meeting? I didn't think I was even allowed to go, but I went anyway because I wanted my mother to talk to me.

I walked through the doors and started crying. In public. I never did that. Especially not without a specific reason. The few members already there came over and gave me big hugs. They told me every single other member came in just like me. They handed me literature. I didn't have to say anything.

The meeting opened. I heard something about becoming irritable and unreasonable without knowing it. *That's me!* And then something about no unhappiness too great to be lessened. *I'll stick around and see if that could be me.* We closed with the serenity prayer. I'd heard it before, and the familiarity soothed me.

For the first time in a really long time, I felt calm. Calm, I drove home. Calm, I ate an apple with my mother. And then Gatlin called. And I was calm. For five minutes. And then I couldn't find that peace I'd been holding onto since the meeting, so I went to another meeting.

I heard something about being powerless. *I guess that's me.* And something about a searching and fearless moral inventory. *I'll steer clear of that for now.*

That afternoon, Gatlin and I went on a date. "You know, you're better when you go to those meeting things."

"Thanks! I heard this great prayer while I was there: God, grant me the serenity to accept—"

"—what I can't change and change the things I can. Yeah, I've heard it before. Actually, I found it on the football field in high school and put it on my keychain."

He got some of the words wrong. That bothered me. "And the wisdom to know the difference…"

"Yeah, I don't really get that. See, we're stuck in traffic right now, but I can't accept that. I refuse to accept the traffic this bad."

Wow, okay, so that was *not* the definition of the serenity prayer. He can't *choose* what to accept and what to change.

And then I understood. *I* couldn't choose either. I couldn't sit in the passenger seat and lecture him on the serenity prayer and pretend I knew it any better than he did. I would never change his mind. Ever. So what would be the point? I'd just become angry and irritable, and my sense of calm would be gone.

I realized my part in everything. That time he told me I wasn't allowed to go out in public without a bra on, *I* tried to change his thinking. How arrogant of me! That time he told me I *had* to make sweet potato pie for Thanksgiving, *I* tried to change his thinking. And when I couldn't, I either ignored that fact, fought him harder, or thought I could eventually change that particular discrepancy. I told myself I would never, ever, ever do any of those again. And then, of course, within twenty minutes of talking to him, I did, but that was longer than ever before. Progress over perfection.

Tissues

"Abigail, every time you've called me in this relationship, you've been crying. I don't like that. I don't like hearing you cry."

Tina was right, and I think she was frustrated with me. How could I still be with someone who clearly did not make me happy? There was nothing she could've said or done that would've convinced me to leave Gatlin, though.

She was right. I cried at least three hours every day for the past couple months. Still, I didn't see that as a sign to get out. Our relationship would get better. It had to. I deserved better, and that "better" would come from him. It would.

When she and I met for lunch one day, she gave me a box of tissues to keep in my car. She was so sensible. She always took care of me when I didn't have the sense to do it myself.

To Love is To Control (V)

"When I told you to ask me out this morning, that was a hint."

"What are you talking about? We just saw each other yesterday all day at the beach!"

"Last week, I specifically asked you whether going to the beach on Tuesday would affect us seeing each other our regular times on Monday and Wednesday. You said, 'It shouldn't.' I asked because your answer affected my response to your invitation."

"You got to see me yesterday. I don't understand why you're upset."

"I'd rather see you more often than once a week, no matter how long it is. It feels like you're setting aside time for me and then saying, 'Now, she should be happy about that,' but it's not like you actually want to spend time with me. Which is fine, but just don't say you're going to see me and then don't."

"I'm busy, and you know it. I set aside all of yesterday, so I have to work today."

"Monday came and went, and you were too tired to even communicate with me, which is, again, fine, but you'd said you'd see me despite the beach trip. I let it go because I'm trying to be understanding of your long work hours on the weekends, but then don't suggest seeing me when you can't. And now today is Wednesday, and you said the trip shouldn't affect me seeing you, and now it is."

"Abigail, I don't understand why you're so upset. It doesn't matter how much time I spend with you; you want more. If I see you one day, you're happy, and if I don't see you the next, you're unhappy."

"It's not about seeing you. It's about me reserving the time to see you like we'd agreed and then you not following through. Do you remember saying you could see me on Monday and Wednesday?"

"Yes."

"So, what happened?"

"My friend is busy, and his girlfriend understands and supports him. She knows he's busy. I'm busy, too."

———

"Dinner Friday night?"

"Hmmm . . . I don't know. . . . I might be super busy or tired. I'm a very busy girl, you know. I might not have time. . . ."

"How am I supposed to want to do anything nice for you if you're always so mean? There's no positive reinforcement, and I don't like your jabby attitude."

—

Bzz. Bzz. Bzz.

"Is that your dad?"

"Yeah, he wants us to take a picture."

Bzz.

"Like right now, during Valentine's Day dinner?"

Bzz. Bzz.

"Yeah, he says taking it after is just an excuse to not take it right now."

Bzz. Bzz. Bzz. Bzz. Bzz.

"Gatlin, your dad is halfway across the country. What would happen if we didn't take the picture?"

"I don't know. I don't even want to think about it. Let's just take the picture and get it over with."

Bzz.

—

"Nobody understands what I've gone through."

"If you don't like your life, then why don't you just move out? You have a job."

"No."

"Why not?"

"Because I'm not moving out until I can support a family."

"Okay. How much do you think you need to make to do that?"

"A hundred and fifty thousand dollars a year."

"You're going to live with your dad until you earn a hundred and fifty thousand dollars per year?"

"Yes."

"Do you know how hard that is?"

"It's not hard because we have a plan, and I just need to follow it exactly so nothing goes wrong. You need to support me. My dad is really smart. He knows what he's talking about. You should talk to him, and he'll help you with your life, too."

Hair

On our third date, Gatlin showed up with the worst haircut I'd ever seen. Only the top of his head had a little bit of hair; the rest was bald. He didn't even have the decency to cover it up with a baseball cap. I spent the next three weeks reminding myself that it was just a haircut, he really was cute, and bad hair wasn't a reason to break it off. I offered to give him the name of a good hair salon, but he insisted he knew of a better place, and the bad haircut had been just a last-minute thing anyway.

After a few weeks, it grew out. For the next three or four months, he had amazing hair and was as cute as anything. Every time I looked at him, I was glad I had pushed through.

Then one morning, he showed up at a workout, proud as a peacock, quite literally strutting. My heart sank. My eyes stung. He'd gotten that same haircut. *His* haircut, as he reminded me, and any girl who didn't like it obviously didn't like him.

Had I really turned into one of those girls who try to fix a guy? Who try to tailor their boyfriends to their liking? What was my issue? Why did I care so much? It was just hair! Gatlin could do whatever he wanted to; it was his body, his hair.

But it's the fact that I'd go to the nail salon, and upon seeing gold as an option, opt to get my nails painted his favorite color. It's the fact that when I showered and wondered if I should shave my legs, I would because that's what he preferred. It's the fact that I'd save wearing his favorite shirt for our date. It's the fact that I'd wear the ring he got me every day because I knew how happy that made him. It's the fact that every choice I came across, I chose the one that would please him more.

I could argue that I was changing myself for him, but I think of it as his opinions having weight in my decisions. I wasn't going to dye my hair, so I never asked what color hair he liked. However, I was already getting my nails done; I just didn't know what color. I was already debating shaving my legs; I just let his taste become a contributing factor. I already owned the shirt; I just didn't know when to wear it.

I wanted to show him that I listened to him, remembered his preferences, and acted upon them, even when he wasn't around. I wanted him to know he meant more to me than a nail color, leg hair, a shirt, a ring, and all other trivialities. Apparently, I meant less to him than a haircut.

Insecure vs. Confident

Insecure Abigail screams in anger, tears rolling down her cheeks. How could she have held tight for so long to someone who treated her so poorly? How could she have let this happen, only to have it end on his terms? Insecure Abigail wanted Gatlin to come crawling back into her arms just to send him away, to make him feel her pain, to make him regret the things he'd said and the things he hadn't done, to make him hear those sad country songs and relate.

But Confident Abigail just laughs. She laughs at the absurdity of it all. Who on this earth would have the audacity to say to his girlfriend, "You know, I wouldn't cry if you broke up with me"? Who says that? But more importantly, who stays with someone who felt the need to say that? Insecure Abigail does, apparently.

Confident Abigail would have laughed and dismissed him from her life, but Insecure Abigail just sobbed. Why couldn't she make him understand? She wasn't asking for a lot—just that he called her when he said he would, visited her when he said he would, and gave her a hug when they were right there together and she said she needed one. It shouldn't have been that hard, especially for a boy who used to exclaim, "I'd do anything for you!" And would reply with "Yes! Anything!" when she challenged him, saying, "Not 'anything' . . ." So Insecure Abigail continued to hope, to cry, to lower expectations.

Maybe it was the fact that heads turned when Gatlin and Abigail walked into a room together. Confident Abigail scorned Insecure Abigail for forgetting that she could turn heads all by herself. Maybe it was the flowers Gatlin brought on Valentine's Day—never mind that Abigail already had too many roses from her own garden. Maybe it was his big, strong arms—never mind the fact that he stopped putting them around her, even when she cried and asked for a hug. Maybe it was the way he stared at her and told her she was so incredibly beautiful—never mind the fact that anyone on the street could have told her the exact same thing. Or maybe it was because he took her out to eat—though it didn't matter that when he asked, and she suggested Panda Express, he drove them to Chipotle without another word.

Whatever the reason, the day before, Insecure Abigail clung to Gatlin like he was her one true love and there was no one else for her, so Confident Abigail met him at Panera for a date. It was innocent enough: they talked, held hands, read an elementary physics book.

Gatlin proudly told Confident Abigail he'd created a schedule. She opened his notebook, and upon seeing the schedule, her heart sank into her stomach. There were his two sixteen-hour shifts cut back to eight hours. But where was studying? Wasn't that supposed to take the place of all this missed work instead of fishing? Then, there was mixed martial arts, starting at six—the reason they couldn't see each other at all on Tuesdays or Thursdays, unless his dad told him, like today, to go see her to cheer himself up. And there are Abigail's scheduled times: Monday lunch, Wednesday lunch, Friday night date. Maybe now he could stick to those days.

But what about everything else? What about his other two to three workouts a day he claimed to do? What about coding? Or his new business? Sure, scattered here and there were a vague "work" or "work out," but it didn't cover nearly all that he claimed he did. And there were empty four-hour chunks of time everywhere!

But Confident Abigail knew better than to say anything. She knew Gatlin was stressed. She knew she couldn't control him or his schedule, so she contented herself with a nod and a "Cool." She decided to relax. He'd made unexpected time for her, after all. Did it matter that he seemed quiet and emotionally unavailable—a change from the beginning of their relationship? It didn't have to—it would matter only if she cared to let it bother her. Propping her bare feet on his lap, Confident Abigail let him admire her nails—painted gold, his favorite color—and she let him touch her feet gingerly, massaging them.

And then he tickled her foot. She tried to pull away, but he held tighter. She said, "Stop!" but the involuntary giggle and smile told him to continue. Memories flooded her mind of all the times she'd told him she didn't like to be tickled. If he couldn't respect this simple thing, what *would* he respect? If he couldn't hear that she didn't like this, would he ever hear her? If he couldn't understand "no means no," whether regarding tickling, sex, or sweet potato pancake, could she really trust him? What point was there to a relationship without even rudimentary trust?

"Gatlin, if you tickle me again, I *will* break up with you."

"But you were smiling."

"I don't care. I didn't like it, and I told you to stop."

Confident Abigail knew there was a nicer way to put it—less demanding, less final, less threatening, less controlling. But this was her boundary. She hoped he'd understand. She hoped he'd realize how much it hurt her and stop. She hoped they would resolve at least this one issue.

She got more lemonade and sat in the booth beside him. After about twenty minutes of sitting in silence, Gatlin tickled her side. Confident Abigail got up, gathered her trash, threw it away, and came back to the table to get her purse.

"I thought we were just talking about feet."

"I didn't say, 'Don't tickle my feet.' I said, 'Don't tickle me.'" But Confident Abigail knew Insecure Abigail wouldn't forgive her for breaking it off over such a small misunderstanding, so Confident Abigail stayed.

When Gatlin ended it the next day, Insecure Abigail broke down. Didn't Confident Abigail know that she just needed to cry? Gatlin wouldn't have listened to anything she'd asked, but he'd still be around. He'd only meant to make her smile.

Smile?! Confident Abigail knew there were so many ways to make people smile—and with joy, at that.

Another Interview

When I think about an interview I had in February, guilt consumes me. Everyone thinks I failed at my truck driving dream. They believe the industry turned me away, but it didn't. I gave up on it. I tell people, "I quit my job, and then everything fell apart, so I moved to Mexico," but that's a lie.

Everything did fall apart, but not in the way I let them think. I had a job offer. The day Gatlin broke up with me, I had a chance to start my career, but I didn't take it. I couldn't. I couldn't let myself and others keep believing that I was still willing to wait two years to be a long-distance driver.

The truth was that I wasn't willing to do office work in the hopes of achieving the dream I'd built over the years. I wanted to be a truck driver. Yes, that part was true. That's all I'd thought about doing. I didn't know what else to do with my life. I loved driving; I loved feeling badass; I loved having a skill that not many others had. But did I love the industry?

Did I have it in my heart to stick it out in an office for two years? To arrive at an office job an hour away from home at seven in the morning? To get there at five in the morning if they needed me? Did I care enough about this dream to accept a demanding job? To live for those few moments I'd get to back up a trailer? Was I willing to give up time and money to make the industry my life? To learn the ins and outs of it all?

The answer was no. I had lied to everyone; I had even lied to myself. I'd thought I could do it. I'd thought I'd want it. Right up to the very last moment when the company's road tester told me I was set to start the following Monday. That's when I saw my life flash before my eyes: endless days in an office; no more early morning workouts; no more time to cry.

Those days, I cried all the time. At work. At home. With my boyfriend. I didn't want to cry at this new job. Not when they were doing me a favor. They'd created the job for me, anticipating my acceptance into the company.

Was it possible to feel grateful for the opportunity and stuck at the same time? Was it possible to want to do it with all my heart and know it wasn't right? Why didn't I know it wasn't right in December, during my first interview with them? Why had it taken me until February to figure it out? Was it possible that I finally knew what it felt like to be stuck in a situation?

I didn't know for sure I'd feel stuck. I might've loved it. I might've bonded with my coworkers. I might've found my purpose. But I didn't think so. I didn't think my calling was in an office of a trucking company. As much as I would have liked everyone else to believe I was willing to do it, I couldn't pretend. Not for two years. Not for the hopes of this dream my whole city knew about now.

Because of my article in the paper,[2] the entire trucking industry and most of Richmond knew. They all knew I wanted to be a truck driver. They knew I was advocating for the Drive-SAFE Act. They knew I had my CDL and was too young to cross state lines. But they didn't know that I didn't care anymore. I didn't want to admit to myself that this thing I thought I wanted, this thing that had become my identity, was no longer me. If I'd gotten a job those few months I'd been desperate, truck driving might've become my life. I might've enjoyed it. I'll never really know.

But I didn't get a job. The one presented to me in February had been too late—I didn't care about trucking anymore—but I didn't have a good reason to turn the job down. I didn't have a backup plan. There was nothing else I was going to do instead. I was simply going away from what I'd built for myself over the past two years.

How could I explain it without sounding like a princess? Like the stereotypical millennial who isn't motivated enough to work for success? Maybe I cared too much about

---

[2] *One big roadblock to my chosen career,* pg.169

my image. But what would people say if they knew? Would they judge me even more? Or would they say, "Good, that was a dumb career path anyway"?

I gave up. I had no excuse. I closed that chapter of my life when I had the perfect opportunity to open it back up. Part of me rejoices in my strength to turn away, but the other part feels nothing but shame. I lied to my whole community, but I didn't mean to. I thought I'd been telling the truth.

A Visit to D.C.

The day after the interview for the job I declined and the day after Gatlin sent me a break-up text, I could not stop crying. Actually, the crying part wasn't too different from the last month or so of the relationship, but early that morning, my mother left for a five-day trip to Puerto Vallarta, Mexico.

I texted my aunt, who's always supportive, especially during times of crisis, and asked if I could come visit. My boyfriend just broke up with me.

"Yes, yes, yes!" came her response.

She was still at work, but I was welcome to come up to D.C. and hang outside on their porch. When her girls got out of school, I could pick them up if I wanted. I did.

"Oh, hi, Abigail," Messina, a middle-schooler, said as she climbed into the backseat of my car. "Thanks for picking us up."

"No problem. Thanks for letting me be here."

"Wait, why are you here again? Not that it's a problem. . . ."

"Oh, um, my boyfriend broke up with me." I tried, and failed, to stop a tear from rolling down my cheek.

"Oh . . . I'm sorry. . . ."

We waited for Dee, who was in high school, to get to the car. When she got in, she said, "This is such a wonderful surprise! It's so great to see you! What brings you up?"

"Oh, um, your mother said it was okay. Gatlin broke up with me." Again, another tear I attempted to contain.

"Oh . . . I'm sorry to hear that."

"Yeah, it's okay. So how were y'all's days at school?"

Dee and Messina proceeded to tell me about their days: tests, homework, tennis. When we got back to their house, we talked a bit, but they had homework to do. I waited until almost 7 at night, but my aunt still wasn't home, so I thought I'd better head back home. I hadn't been planning on spending the night.

About ten minutes into my drive, I got a call from Aunt Jo.

"Hi, Sweetie Pie, where are you?"

"Oh, I'm driving back. . . . It's getting late. . . . Thank you for letting me come up!"

"All the way to Richmond?"

"Yeah."

"Are you okay? Are you sure that's safe?"

"Yeah, I'll be okay."

I think she heard me sniffle because she said, "Come back. I don't want you on the road when you're emotional."

Well, I wasn't going to argue with that, so I turned around.

When I got back, Dee and Aunt Jo were waiting for me with huge hugs. I sat down on a stool at their kitchen island while Jo prepared food and Dee made me ginger peach longevity tea. She remembered that I found it had incredible emotional healing powers when I was down.

I told them about all the ways I felt that I kept trying to lower my expectations and standards and how I just didn't seem to be doing anything right. I cried about everything that didn't make sense, and like the sympathetic aunt she is, Aunt Jo took my side. She got angry for me, she turned it into a lesson for Dee.

"Where's your mom?"

"She left for Mexico this morning."

"What's she doing down there?"

"Do you know the Dukes? They're our friends who live in North Carolina. Waylon's the one who was born the same day as me. Anyway, Gretchen, the mom, her mom, Rena, died over the summer. We went to her celebration of life in Wisconsin, and now they're having one in Mexico because Rena has a condo down there. It's on the water, and you can see dolphins from the balcony. She'd been to Afton Mountain a couple times, and I've been to her place in Puerto Vallarta once a few years ago. So anyway, my mother is there now."

"Why didn't you go with her?"

"I thought I was going to be working."

"That's where you need to be. You need good weather and good tacos right now. Dee, find the next flight to Puerto Vallarta from Washington, D.C."

"But I don't have any of my things."

"Buy it all down there. Do you have your passport?"

"No."

"Drive down to Richmond early tomorrow morning and then come up and take the flight. Dee should be able to find a nonstop from here."

Dee pulled up the next cheapest flight, and I bought the ticket.

The next morning, I drove back home, rushed to pack a suitcase, got a text saying my flight from D.C. was cancelled, bought another ticket out of Richmond, and left.

Stay Funny

Between my second and final leg to Mexico, I received a text from my mother with the following instructions:

1. When you walk out of the airport, take a left and walk across the footbridge over the interstate. Walk past the taxis. Do not take a taxi.

2. At the other end of the footbridge, call an Uber to Estudio Café. That is where we're staying.

3. If Estudio Café is open, tell the owners you are my daughter, and they will show you where we are sleeping.

4. Code to the condo where our hosts are staying is 1234. Bri and kids are staying there tonight, but Gretchen and I are going to a performance.

I walked out of the airport, passed all the taxi drivers calling out to me, and made it across the footbridge. Upon opening the Uber app, I found I couldn't take an Uber because I wasn't connected to the Mexican cell towers.

A man approached me, asking if I needed a taxi, but I declined. My mother had told me not to take a taxi. I wasn't sure why she'd said it, but I was going to follow her directions. In eighth grade, an exchange student from Ecuador had told us how the taxi drivers kidnap their passengers after intoxicating them with some kind of drug through touch. I wasn't in Ecuador, but maybe something similar could happen here. I didn't know.

I decided instead to approach a stranger and say in Spanish, "My phone isn't working, but I need to get to Estudio Café. Do you know how I can connect to the towers?"

"For twenty dollars, I'll take you."

"No, no, that's okay. Thanks."

Three men now surrounded me, and I noticed another one, who had walked across the footbridge with me, glancing over in our direction. It was time to head back to the airport. Retracing my steps, I crossed the bridge, passed the taxis, and walked into the airport, sitting down at a table where someone handed me a menu.

"Oh, is this a restaurant?"

"Yes."

No one was sitting at any of the tables, and it was getting really late. "Do I have to order something to sit here?"

"Well, it is a restaurant. . . ."

"Oh, okay." I got up.

I stood near the restaurant, watching all the people pass. They all seemed to know where they were going, or at least knew what they were looking for. Teenage girls were texting on their phones. How come their phones were working, but mine wasn't? I asked in the customs line, but they were also clueless. I decided to just stand there until my mother realized I couldn't get home.

A man approached me—the same man who'd crossed the bridge and watched me explain my situation to the sidewalk strangers. "Excuse me, your Uber is waiting outside for you."

"I didn't order an Uber."

"Uh . . . I don't know how to say . . ."

"You can say it in Spanish if you want," I assured him in Spanish.

"Yes? You speak Spanish? Well, I heard you talking, and an Uber is willing to take you because he lives near where you're going."

"Oh, that's okay, but thank you. I can't connect to the Uber app."

"I work at the airport. Here's my name." He flashed me his airport name badge. "You don't have to, but I just wanted to let you know. I'll see you out there."

I realized that my mother was most likely not going to notice my absence for another six hours at least. My mother's family has historically prided itself on giving children freedom. This meant I'd been free to get my CDL and buy myself chips, but I'd also been free to fail a history midterm and navigate a Mexican airport alone. Besides, customs could take forever, and plane schedules are unpredictable.

I also realized, however, that taking this airport employee up on his offer would be breaking every single stranger danger warning I'd ever heard in my entire life. I was not supposed to talk to strangers, let alone in a foreign country, and I was certainly not supposed to take a ride from—not even said stranger, but a stranger to the person offering me a ride. But I could see in his earnest face that he just wanted to help. I was a young girl close to tears, and he wanted to help. Every bone in my body told me not to go, but my heart said that most people have very good, very pure intentions.

"Okay."

"Yes? Let's go. He's over here."

We walked past the taxis again.

"So, my mother told me not to take the taxis," I said in Spanish. "Why would she say that?"

"Two reasons. One, they're more expensive, and two, they're more dangerous."

"More dangerous than going in a stranger's car?"

The man laughed. "You have a point there."

I proceeded to tell him that my boyfriend had broken up with me and I was in Mexico because my life was falling apart. Because I had no one else in the world, and because

I was so relieved to have someone, anyone, on my side, I laughed when I said it. I wanted to be the smiling, carefree woman with a big hat in the movies that shows up to a tropical island when everything falls apart.

"I want to tell you: Stay funny."

I didn't feel particularly funny. In fact, despite my laughter, I was close to tears and lost in a foreign country. One of the two people I'd communicated with most in the past few months had decided to never talk to me again, and the other was at a performance with her friend. I couldn't blame my mother, though. We'd talked earlier that week about how she doesn't worry about me and how it forces me to act and think for myself and how I'm somewhat grateful for it. But how in the world did this airport worker think I was funny?

We got to my "Uber," and the driver asked me to put my destination into Google Maps. The "Uber" driver put my bag in his trunk and opened the door for me. I turned to the airport worker, my one friend in this country, and waved, whispering "*¡Gracias!*" He turned with a smile as I got into the backseat of the red car.

My "Uber" driver made sure I could see his phone screen with the directions during the car ride, but all I could think about was how this was how I'd go out. No boyfriend to worry about me. No friends to know I'd left the country.

No mother suspecting anything went wrong until hours too late. How would she even find me when she realized I was gone? I started crying. I wanted to text Gatlin, but I knew that even if I could and even if we were still together, he wouldn't care. There wasn't anything left for me to do but let the tears fall and watch the scenery. The greenery would've pleased my eye more in a less stressful scenario.

The "Uber" driver started veering from Google's directions. I hadn't noticed, but he wanted to make sure I knew he was just taking a shortcut. He kept pointing out the route he planned on taking, and I kept repeating, "Okay." I just wanted him to be quiet and let me calm down, but I know he only wanted me to trust him. I did, actually. I'm not sure I ever distrusted him; I'd distrusted the entire situation but not any person in particular.

He dropped me off in front of Estudio Café, and I gave him twenty US dollars, although we hadn't discussed a price. I assumed it was fair since the previous man had offered it. Besides, that's all the cash I had. At first, he frowned, but then lit up. I later realized that twenty pesos would have been the equivalent of one US dollar, but twenty US dollars was more than three times the cost of an Uber ride to the airport, and, of course, the drivers don't see all that money. He'd taken a risk on me, and I on him, and we'd both parted the better for it.

I saw Estudio Café's hours: 8:30 A.M. to 3 P.M. It was currently 8 P.M. Couldn't my mother have read the sign? I moved on to step four of her instructions: the code to the condo. The location hadn't been disclosed, only the code. I walked to the water and recognized the marina from five years ago. Stored in the depths of my memory, a blue building stood out. I'd try that one first, and then start at the beginning of the row of condos with the code, if the blue one failed.

The code worked on the first building!

My stomach grumbled. I'd consumed only a can of Pringles and some sweet tea all day—to settle my stomach on the plane. Carrying my light but bulky suitcase, I climbed fifty-one steps: seventeen for each flight. I remembered the condo being high up, but how high, I couldn't say. I passed a metal gate, which seemed a familiar landmark and indicator. I couldn't remember which condo was Gretchen's mother's. Both were dark and quiet. I tried one, then the other. Nothing.

I walked back to the third floor, to an open condo door, and knocked.

"Come in. I'm not getting up," came a gruff voice, out of my sight.

I stayed where I was, on the threshold. "Hi . . . um . . . Do you know where Rena used to live?"

"Right upstairs." The voice stayed true to its word and didn't come into view.

"Which one?"

"Either one. It's all one big condo."

"Oh, well, I don't think they're there."

"I think I know where they are. Go up and try again first."

I lugged my suitcase back up the stairs and knocked. Again, no answer. Holding my suitcase so it wouldn't bang on the steps, I went back downstairs.

"They're not there," I reported back to the voice.

"Try Eddie's. They might be eating dinner there. Go all the way down the sidewalk. All the way. It comes in and then keeps going. Go past that to the end."

"Okay, thank you."

I took thirty-four steps down with my last-minute suitcase. I turned to the left with the water on my right. I walked down the cobblestone sidewalk. As soon as I couldn't follow his directions anymore, I stopped at every restaurant, asking for Eddie's. At the fifth restaurant, I saw a girl who looked familiar. Although I'd only met her once four months prior, I was pretty sure I recognized her. I turned to the waiters and said, glancing in the girl's direction, "I think I'm looking for them. Can I go in?"

After a waiter nodded, I climbed over the low chain

indicating the boundary of the restaurant. Almost in tears again from hunger and exhaustion, I sat in the vacant seat of the table for four. The girl, Daisy, and her mom, Bri, were accompanied by someone I didn't recognize; she must've been Daisy's friend my mother mentioned a couple days ago.

"You found us! Did you like the scavenger hunt we left for you?"

"Hi. . . . When's my mom gonna be back?"

Daisy's dad came back from paying the bill. Apparently, they had texted me in a group chat when they'd left for dinner.

As we headed back to the condo, I recounted my night's adventures. The family kept asking me to retell the part involving the voice on the third floor, as if the interaction amazed them; yet everyone glazed over the incredible survival of accepting a ride, as an American, from a random Mexican on the side of the road with no accountability. It seems that every chance they have, people are good to each other, and I, like many people, often forget this.

Bri made me a quesadilla while we waited for my mother and Gretchen, but for some reason, I couldn't eat it. Soon, my mom showed up.

"Hi, sweetie! How are you doing?" My mother came over to give me a big hug.

"I'm hungry."

"Barracuda's still open!" Gretchen chimed in.

"Do you want to go there?"

I nodded.

Why Would I Ever Leave?

The morning after arriving in Puerto Vallarta, I sat in Estudio Café enjoying breakfast with my mother. I took in the warm air and my beautiful surroundings of bright green plants on a white patio overlooking the marina. And the burrito! It satisfied cravings I didn't know I had; the egg and cheese were so light and fluffy—not to mention the delicate tortilla casing.

"Why would I ever leave?"

My mother continued to eat her burrito, letting me have my moment.

How could I leave a place that made me feel like a movie star on vacation? Or one of those well-to-do people in the movies without a care in the world?

And on the flip side, what did I have to go back to? I'd left a rainy, forty-degree Richmond and a snowy Washington, D.C. I'd left a home scattered with little reminders of Gatlin: the wilting flowers he'd brought on Valentine's Day; the necklace he'd given me for my birthday; the ring he'd thought was real emerald and diamond, with which he'd tried to propose after only a month of dating. All these items would be there to remind me that Gatlin wasn't with me, except at the early morning workouts, where I'd see his terrible haircut and his arrogant but playful exchanges with his friend, and where, at least on the surface, nothing would be wrong.

So, again, I repeated, "Why would I ever leave?"

Since I was closer to my revelation but not quite there, my mother left me alone with my thoughts. I had nothing at home, yet the most wonderful weather in Mexico. I looked at my mother, posing the same question but this time with more seriousness, and she replied, "You don't have to."

I shrugged off her statement, as she can be a little too carefree, but the next morning, I felt the same air, saw the same view, tasted the same perfect burrito, and again the question haunted me.

"Why would I ever leave?"

And so, it came to be that I would rent our friends' condo above Estudio Café until the spirit moved me elsewhere.

Homesick

I missed Chaha when I lived in Mexico. She knew I had sensitive skin. She knew that at fifteen, I cried the first time she waxed my eyebrows. She knew I still cried when she threaded them. She was the one who told me that threading lasts longer than plucking and has a better shape than waxing.

Chaha had tissues. And thin, white thread. Not like the thick, red thread Max had. He was the only one in all of Puerto Vallarta that did threading. Or at least, he claimed he did. Before he started, I saw him behind a tall bookshelf in the mirror as he flipped through an instruction book. Not like Chaha. She told me every girl in Nepal has to learn a skill, and she chose threading.

Chaha had me lie down and guided my hair so it gently fell away from my eyebrows. Not like Max. He had me sit in a corner so I couldn't back away and used rough hands to push my hair aside.

Chaha called me "dear" or Abigail. Max didn't care to know my name. He told me I needed an appointment a week in advance, but Chaha never turned me away.

After Chaha, my eyebrows became my best feature, and

I felt like a pampered princess. After Max, I never wanted to go back, and I resolved to never leave Chaha again.

When my mother visited me in Mexico, she handed me a Ziploc bag with an index card and small, white thread. Paraphrased, the note says: *Chaha said he's using the wrong thread and you have sensitive skin. This spool should last over a year. Keep in bag, or it will tangle.*

Except for the fact that Chaha sent me love from a different country, the new thread didn't help.

Living Up to Perfection

Gatlin used to think I was perfect. He insisted I was, even when I tried to remind him that no human is capable of perfection. He didn't believe me, so I began to believe him. He used to tell me every day that I was perfect.

So, what changed? Wasn't I still beautiful? Wasn't I still smart? Wasn't I still strong? Of course, I was! So, why was I not still perfect in his eyes? What had I done to destroy that image?

Of course, it's foolish to aim for perfection. It's unattainable—everyone says so. But why? If I continue with intentions to do right, why am I no longer worthy of the compliment? Maybe it's the definition of "right" that defines perfection. What's right in my eyes is not in his.

To me, it's right to state my preferences, but to him, it's a personal attack. To me, it's right to say, "I don't want to be treated that way; it's not okay," but to him, it's right for me to stay silent and agreeable.

Because of these differences in perception of "right," perfection and its attributes change by the person. What's perfect to me isn't to him. And what's imperfect to us may be perfect to someone else, thus the achievement of complete and unwavering perfection becomes impossible, simply by the contradictory nature of man. And maybe that is why it's not up to the human race to define or even attempt perfection, but up to a higher power as defined by the individual.

Pizza

"Oh, um, y'all can have some if y'all want." I'd just brought home a large pizza from the restaurant next door. It would've been rude to eat in front of guests, who were friends with one of the sisters I rented the condo from.

Neither mother nor son responded in a manner that suggested they wanted a slice, so I ate the entire pizza in about five minutes.

"Oh, wow, you ate that whole thing?" The mother laughed.

I shrugged. Ideally, fruits and vegetables should've been added to my Mexico diet of tacos, Cheez-Its, grape juice, pizza, and Coca-Cola, but at least I was hungry again.

Married to the Ocean

At age twelve, I went to Honduras and met a free-spirited woman. She showed my mother and me the best place to snorkel with the fish among the coral. On the way back from snorkeling, she recounted her past. She was in an abusive relationship; she packed her bags for Honduras and moved there, not knowing a single word of Spanish; she found a plastic ring in the beach's waves and declared herself "married to the ocean."

I remember admiring her absolute courage in moving to a foreign country. I admired her ability to learn a new language and speak it fluently within two years. I imagined the confidence it would take to do something like that and the freedom to claim the entire powerful ocean as your spouse. To me, it was the ultimate oneness with nature. The ocean and sand and fish fulfilled her earthly needs. She didn't need anything more, nor was she searching for something else.

My goal was to embody the strength she emanated. To know I'd packed my bags for Mexico the way she did for Honduras helped me appreciate the ocean and feel peace wash over me with each wave flow around my feet.

Carey

After breaking up with his girlfriend of two years, a nineteen-year-old boy went to Mexico for a week. He wanted to drink beer and sleep around. No one would blame him if he did. No one would wonder why. No one would even blink twice. So, what stopped him? What could have been so powerful as to stop a brokenhearted, horny teenage boy from numbing his pain with alcohol and sex in a foreign country with virtually no repercussions? With his grandparents as his only supervision, he was basically free to do whatever he wants whenever he wants.

Rational reasons to refrain from such a rampage would include fear of an STD, and the belief that it's just not right. But what does "right" really mean? Who declared it immoral to fuck strangers? Who decided what was right and what was wrong? Did those two "rational" reasons for abstaining actually get to the heart of the issue? And what was the issue, if one existed at all?

I played cards with Carey's grandmother in Mexico, and she introduced us one night at dinner. Bored, we met up a couple days later for tacos. At dinner, I laughed so hard I almost peed my pants. In an instant, life had become funny again. I ordered a water and received an orange-lime lemonade drink I couldn't pretend to enjoy. He ordered a Coke and received a Pepsi, which wasn't weird until the waiter handed other customers Coke bottles. Neither one of us got mad; that's just the Mexico life. Then I thought of Gatlin: he would've gotten mad, and I never truly laughed so hard with him.

Throughout dinner, we mainly talked about Carey's ex-girlfriend: what happened, how he felt, how she acted after, how he wanted to act. Everything came out. He had no reason to be afraid I'd tell her or her friends, or that rumors would spread about what he was doing, how he felt in the moment. He was safe.

With a walk along the beach, we extended our time together. Every strand of the conversation returned to his ex. I didn't mind. I'd been in that same place not too long ago. Actually, I was still there, but his ever-present feelings came refreshingly before mine that night. I'd grown tired of my own emotions and had long been ready to accept someone else's. After our walk, we sat in the sand, watching the waves under the moonlight. Carey confessed that he'd gotten an invitation from a couple cute university girls to go to a party that night, where he definitely could've gotten laid.

I told him he could go. I knew how much he wanted to sleep around, so my encouragement had been genuine. If he needed it like he thought, what kept him from standing up and going? He said he was happy; he didn't need it right then. He was truly in the moment.

I asked about what drove his desire to go on a "rampage" with any girl who was willing. "Revenge."

"Do you want revenge right now while you're looking at the water and feeling the sand on your legs?"

"No."

"So, why do you want revenge?"

"To get peace."

"How would that get you peace?"

"To make her hurt like I'm hurting."

"But isn't the nature of wanting revenge oriented in the past?"

"No, I want revenge in the present, too."

"Because you're thinking about the past?"

"Yes."

"But do you want it when you're thinking about only the water and sand?"

"No."

"Wouldn't that be considered the true present, true peace?"

"Fuck, well, yeah, I guess."

Our conversation went on: I asked a question; he thought about it; he answered. I responded with another question, and the cycle continued. Whatever question I posed, he genuinely put thought into his answer. Every query required such insight on Carey's part that he had no more room to think about his ex—only the waves, the sand, and his soul. Realizations ebbed and flowed with the water: he wanted revenge; he was at peace; he wanted revenge to achieve peace. The fluctuations lessened until he claimed that he honestly and truly felt in his soul that going on a rampage would not solve his emotional problem. It took three hours.

Peace was just a cycle. Yes, we both felt peace in that moment, but I knew in the future we'd be sad again. But then we'd find peace another time, and slowly, the healing process would begin. Peace was to be relished every second it was present.

I had no preconceived notion about what was "right" for Carey's situation. If he wanted sex and concluded that it would help, I had no objection to his taking that resolution into his own hands, assuming all acts to be consensual. I didn't care if his body count increased by ten that night, or if he went home to play Words with Friends with his grandparents. Because he was scheduled to fly back home the next day, I knew I wouldn't see him again. His conclusion was his and his alone to make. Wanting to justify himself, he fought my perspective with an open mind. Nothing kept him from leaving, yet he stayed to ponder the questions posed and to live this last night on the beach. A little before midnight, I realized I needed to get home before all the drivers went to bed, so he ordered me an Uber.

Five days later, he texted me to say I had been right, and he had given my words thought. A rampage would not have solved anything. I had helped. For all I knew, he'd go on a different rampage later. Without a doubt, the feelings would return, and the choice to act upon them or not would be his. I'm not naïve enough to think those three hours changed his actions forever.

Talking about peace helped me channel it, helped me feel it genuinely. Asking questions about peace and its meaning, the meaning of revenge, and the notion of the present reinforced living in the moment. Talking with Carey reminded me to do something I hadn't done in a long time: ask questions. Gatlin never liked all my questions, but with Carey, I remembered the power behind inquisitiveness. I got to know Carey, to understand where he was coming from, and to help him understand what would be good for him in the moment. I had no stake in whether or not he went on a rampage. If that's what would genuinely bring him peace, then that was the solution; if it wasn't, it was good to take a step back from the situation, to find a way to go through life with emotional intention. Questions are the root of all information, and maybe that's why some people are scared of them.

Annual Checkup

People asked a lot of questions. What was I doing in Mexico? What was I doing with my life? Wouldn't my brain deteriorate with no activity? What was my plan? Where did I see myself going? All of these questions were left unanswered because I had no answer. At least, I had none that I saw as socially acceptable or appropriate to bring up in a light, social setting. I didn't even want to tell people I was writing a book because everyone knew someone who was an unpublished "writer." Luckily, the fact of a published op-ed at age eighteen continued to give me confidence, but one article differed greatly from a book. Nevertheless, I kept the book close to my chest; I wanted it to be a surprise for my friends, my family, everyone. However, my silence was met with questions. So many questions and so much judgment.

Sometimes, the truth slipped out. Sometimes, even when I fought to keep it all hidden, the truth was too powerful to contain. I never wanted to make excuses for my behavior or my situation, but sometimes those excuses made themselves known.

In March, about six months after my article was published, the International Foodservice Distributors

Association (IFDA) reached out to see if I would be willing to meet with some of my representatives in Congress about the Drive-SAFE Act and do a mini-interview in front of the IFDA members, who regularly brought up my article. I told them I was in Mexico but willing to make the trip, and they agreed to fly me into Washington, D.C. I decided to use that time in the United States to get an STD test and women's annual checkup, since I was overdue for it.

When I got into the doctor's office, the nurse asked me routine questions, including inquiring about my current medications. I listed my three acne prescriptions: Absorica (a form of Accutane and isotretinoin), birth control, and spironolactone.

"What kind of birth control?"

"I'm not sure. It's the kind with the ingredient for acne."

"Let me check your records to see if it's in there."

"It's not. My dermatologist prescribed it in the fall, and I was last here a couple years ago."

"Your dermatologist prescribed it? That's weird."

"Do they not usually prescribe birth control?"

"No. I'm checking your records."

"It won't be there," I informed her again. It didn't feel so unusual for a dermatologist to prescribe birth control for acne—most girls my age knew it could help with hormonal acne.

The nurse kept questioning me and doubting my story, so I came up with an "acceptable" reason: the seriousness behind not getting pregnant on Accutane.

"Now that makes more sense." She had an implicit "because you're having sex."

Something inside me dropped. *No!* I didn't take birth control so I could be sexually active. My dermatologist had prescribed it before isotretinoin, before I had a boyfriend, before I'd ever kissed anyone. I'd planned on my birth control method being abstinence because that's how I'd always done it previously. Was my taking birth control implicit permission for what happened back in December? I remembered Gatlin's skepticism about my "purity" when he found out I was on birth control, as if birth control's only purpose was to let a guy have unprotected sex. I wanted to tell the nurse that she had gotten it all wrong. I wanted to tell her that everyone had gotten it all wrong. My acne qualified as severe, and my birth control has nothing to do with my sex life. It was never supposed to give permission to anyone for anything.

When the nurse left the room, I couldn't hold it in any longer. Naked except for the provided gown, I hunched over, my chest feeling as though it was caving in. Tears started rolling out. At first, I didn't want the tears to come, but they felt so good, I let them flow. I would cover it up when my doctor came in, but when she finally did, I was too tired to hide anything.

"What's going on? Was it a rape situation, or did you guys accidentally go too far?"

"I don't know," I whispered.

She said, "I find it funny how many people come in here saying they don't know, but *I* know. I'm looking right at you!"

That word is so strong. How could I have been raped if I hadn't physically struggled against him? And what if I genuinely enjoyed making out with him and just didn't want to go that extra step yet? Was it still rape then? What about when I was too ignorant to know how it felt? Too ignorant to know at what point he'd stepped over my boundary? Too ignorant to know that the worry and confusion I felt wasn't right? Did I secretly want it if I never punched him or tried to shove him off me?

But I understood what she meant as I watched how my body moved: convulsing and crying, hunched and scared. She refrained from asking many more details and assured me that sex wasn't supposed to be like that, that it wasn't always like that.

"I'm glad he's not in your life anymore. You'd be surprised how many women don't break up with guys like that."

I didn't have the heart to tell her I wasn't the one to end it.

During my breast exam, the doctor tried to lighten the mood by asking, "So, are you a student?"

I figured she already knew the toughest part of my last year, so I might as well reveal everything. I told her about truck driving, about how I had gotten my CDL and couldn't find a job because of insurance and the federal regulated age being twenty-one. I told her about driving a dump truck that would shut down when I was going forty-five miles an hour. I told her about how my ex and I broke up around the same time I quit my job, and how I said, "I'm done with this," and moved to Mexico.

The doctor was impressed with everything, then laughed when I got to leaving the country. "Of course, you did!" she'd exclaimed. She understood! She almost seemed proud of me. Relief flowed through my body. I could immediately feel myself relax.

There were no questions about my ambitions or what I was doing now in Mexico. There was no judgment about my brain atrophying with no job or schoolwork. There were no questions about how long I'd be in Mexico or my plan for coming back.

There was only understanding. There was only pride in my strength. To her, I wasn't running from my responsibilities but distancing myself from past hurt. She didn't need an explanation for my decision; my story was reason enough.

While that particular doctor felt special in my heart for understanding, I realized that anyone could understand my situation if I allowed myself to be vulnerable enough. There was a time and place to be vulnerable, and her office had both. There needed to be space, and she gave it to me. She was ready to hear my story, but not everyone is when they ask me questions.

Because of this experience, I knew who I wanted to become. I wanted to become the person who asked a question and was ready for any answer. I wanted to become the person who allowed space for healing before and after a vulnerability is revealed. I would be the person who wanted to understand, environment permitting.

Mexican Water

"Something to drink?"

"I'll have water, please."

"Mexican water, no?"

"What?"

"You know what Mexican water is?"

I shook my head.

"Tequila!" A grin and a shoulder shimmy usually followed.

"Oh, no, I'm okay, thanks."

Tequila seemed to be the answer for everything. Eleven in the morning? Tequila. Playing cards? Tequila. Any drink served with a wink? Tequila.

When a few friends came to visit, it did not take long for them to realize I wasn't drinking. Toward the end of their trip, when I still refused to take a sip, the friend of my friend said, "I'm going to come into your room while you're sleeping and pour alcohol down your throat."

If he had actually done that and then offered me a drink the next day, would I still have refused?

How Hard Was It, Really?

Sometimes, when I was distanced from the past, I asked myself if I really, honestly, truly did the best I could. How hard was it, really, to wait a couple days for a response from my boyfriend? To hang around all day Saturday and Sunday for his two twenty-minute breaks to answer his calls? How hard was it, really, to dispel his jealousy when I didn't answer? And how hard was it, really, to wait around for no call? How hard was it, really, to have texts from his dad interrupt our only two or three times together a week? To be told he planned to see me and get stood up? How hard was it, really, to eat where I wanted only when I cried? And to live a life ruled by someone else's dad, and if not his dad, ruled by a boyfriend created in the image of his dad? How hard was it, really, to be there when he wanted me and disappear when he didn't? How hard was it, really, to eat sweet potatoes? To watch my body and observe how it was touched?

And then I remember how it started. Gatlin hadn't expected anything of me; I was already perfect. He was scared to touch me without my permission, scared to talk for fear of driving me away. And then it escalated so quickly, with no end in sight. I could feel his control over my body and soul growing. It wasn't the above that would've been too hard, but the ensuing demands, ones I don't care to remember. When I rose to a challenge, another would present itself.

So now I had to ask myself another question. How hard would it have been, really, to break up with him?

A Letter

A letter for the girl flirting with him now:

I see you watching him the way I used to watch him. I see the way you perk up when he's around, and the way your body lights up when he tells you something. Out here, he's happy and confident, almost easygoing. He's strong and fast. Cute. Winning smile. I know you just can't wait until he asks you out, so you won't listen to me. You'll think you're different from me, so I won't waste my time telling you to say no.

After you say yes, he'll make you feel special. He'll tell you you're the prettiest girl he's ever been on a date with. Yes, even prettier than I am. You'll meet his dad on the second date and not like him, but your new boyfriend doesn't have to be like his dad, right? You work out, you're strong, you'll just wait a little longer to see how it goes. If he gets bad, you'll leave. That's what you'll tell yourself.

Then he'll tell you he loves you, and you'll believe him because he means it. When he says he wants to marry you, he does. He really truly does. You'll think that should be enough, especially when he says he'd do anything to keep you. What he won't tell you is that "anything" is really only anything his dad approves of, but you don't know this, so you decide you're willing to do anything as well.

He'll tell you all his past girlfriends cheated on him, so you determine not to do anything that would make him suspicious. After all, how could you want anyone else when you have him?

You'll tell him you're not ready for sex yet, and he'll say he's perfectly fine with that. He's not in it for that, just you. He says you can take your time. But he'll ask. Every chance he has, he'll ask. And you'll say no because you're still not ready.

You'll think y'all are on the same page, but then he'll do the opposite. It'll be so incredible that you'll believe it was a mistake, a mistake that's made every time he disagrees with you.

Or maybe you're ready to have sex as soon as he is. But I hope that means you also like sweet potato pancakes. And his hand down your pants even after you try to pull it out. And don't argue when his dad says the stock market doubles every seven years and that means putting in twenty thousand dollars every year gets you two hundred and eighty thousand dollars at the end of seven years. I hope you know how to answer every single text and call immediately, even when you're with friends. And that you also know how to be okay when he doesn't call for two days. And I hope you won't mind when he doesn't think you have a reason to be mad about anything.

At workouts, he'll come stand next you. He won't have anything interesting to say, but he'll be there, claiming his territory. Your heart will fall into your stomach, but you won't know why. You won't know why you don't eat much anymore. You might actually kind of like it; you'll be getting the body you've always wanted.

Sometimes, you won't have it in you to be nice. You'll be too hurt. And sad. So, when he approaches and your heart sinks and he blames everything on your attitude, you'll forget that no one has ever, ever, ever had a problem with your "mean" attitude. You'll think it's your fault that he's growing distant, that he's not calling, so you try to do better. Maybe you'll exercise more, just to get some endorphins going. You'll try to see friends, but you see how upset it makes him, so you might stop.

And that six-pack you admire now will sadden you later. Some days you'll feel strong and realize you don't need to put up with him, but when he sees that in your eyes, he'll grab your wrist so tight you can't pull away. You won't be able to physically leave. It'll be just long enough to make you think you don't want to leave but not so long you'll realize what he's doing. The grip will be just long enough to make you realize he's driven you two hours away and that you won't be able to get back without him. Please, don't dream about those abs. Instead, know the physical strength they signify.

And even after you break up, he'll text you. He'll call you. You'll want to call back, but all your friends are telling you not to. They'll tell you that every time they heard from you during the relationship, it was about how sad he was making you, and how mad it made them. You'll want to ignore them, and then they'll ask you, "Did he ever do anything nice for you?" And you'll think. You'll think and think and think. You'll go into the depths of your mind and come up with only two things: he paid for your meals and opened the car door for you.

And then you'll ask yourself why you still want him back. All I can tell you is that hope and control are powerful things, but I can tell you my trick for not responding. I think of the most undeniably malicious thing he's intentionally done and keep it as my mantra when I see him or when he calls and texts. I promise you'll have sundry memories to aid you in that process. Then remember that moment, and tell yourself it's just for today. Just for today you won't respond. Just for today you won't be hurt. Just for today.

You'll see another girl acting like you are now, how I once did, and you'll want to send her this letter. But you'll also know that it wouldn't do any good, so you don't. You just try to move on with your life. Sometimes you'll cry, sometimes you'll miss him (God only knows why, but you will), sometimes you'll feel on top of the world and think you were being ridiculous, and most of the time, you'll just be numb.

But one day, we'll be fine. We'll be ten times stronger than we were before him. We'll never forget, but we won't hurt as much. One day, we're both going to be okay.

P.S. Months after the break-up, you'll go for a walk with him. And you'll remind him of a specific night, and he'll tell you he doesn't regret what he did. Like that should make you feel better. It won't. And then he'll want to get back together. He'll tell you he's changing, and you'll send him the number to an abusive partner hotline. The next day, he'll ask you out to lunch, and that's when you'll realize that he must've been dropped on his head as a baby.

My Mexico Adventures

When I got back from Mexico, all my friends wanted to hear how it was. What did I do? Did I have a job? Did I volunteer? Did I have a fling with a cute Mexican guy? My unfortunate responses: nothing, no, no, and no.

It was hard for them to envision doing absolutely nothing for three months, but that's what I did. And it was the best thing for me. When I felt like crying, I'd walk along the beach and cry. I'd let every ugly feature come out: snot, tears, red face. Because I was so far from home, so far from everything and everyone I knew, nothing mattered anymore. I had the freedom to cry all day. About anything. Usually, I cried about Gatlin, but sometimes it'd be about how I had no friends. Or maybe, I stubbed my toe, and I just couldn't stop the tears from escaping.

Mexico gave me the freedom to be unapologetically pathetic. If I wanted to wear pajamas around town, I did it. If I wanted to go out without a bra or underwear on, I did it. Nothing to stop me; no one to care. It was a strange mix of loneliness and independence, and somewhere in the middle, I found myself.

Somewhere in between, I found time to read and write

and play cards with old ladies. I read everything my mother brought down on her monthly check-in visits. I had nothing to do all day but expand my literary knowledge, whether American classics or cheesy romance novels or nonfiction. As my boredom increased, so did my mind's desire to take on a new perspective of the world. Through all that, though, my mind realized it had its own perspective of the world and wanted to share it in the form of this book. These short stories helped transform my negative energy and bad moods into a positive and productive form. This book validated my view. It forced me to face reality, and then allowed me to let go of it all. These events didn't happen to me; they happened to this book. I didn't need to carry them around inside of me anymore, denying their existence.

And because all those emotions exhausted me, I joined retired women at the yacht club Tuesday and Thursday afternoons for a four-hour round of cards. There, I'd enjoy Mexican Coke, popcorn, and the chatter of old ladies. These afternoons reminded me not to take life so seriously. Those women had all gone through their own hardships and lived through it to talk about what font and size and color the new plastic cards should be. They had friends dropping like flies and health problems out the wazoo, yet they managed to continue their small talk about grandchildren and getting their nails done. As to be expected with any group of females, drama always rose to the surface and ebbed away with the next hand. During my time in Mexico, I lived for playing cards with my friends, who all, with the exception of a fifty-five year old, happened to be more than three times my age.

So, when I got back to Richmond, I had no adventures to report. Living in Mexico has such a wild connotation that I felt bad for revealing the uninteresting truth to my friends, but I have no regrets about how I spent my time. I came back to the United States strong and with an understanding and acceptance of who I am. I started working out a couple times a day, writing, and reading to fill the gaps. I'd realized the importance of seeing friends to my mental health, so I tried to arrange a social visit almost every day. I stopped caring that I didn't have an answer to where I was going in life because I realized that it was *my* life, and I was finally taking control over it.

A First, and Hopefully Not a Last

A couple months after I got back from Mexico, I visited some family members on Afton Mountain, our shared vacation place. When I heard we'd be going to the top of the mountain on Saturday night, I hoped I'd get to be in the passenger seat. Everyone knew I had my CDL, so maybe they'd let me take part as an up-close viewer. Because I didn't want to be let down, I didn't tell anyone my desire, so when they told me that *I* would drive the hay-wagon to the top of the mountain that night, my heart soared. This was better than what I'd dreamed of, better than what I wished for as a kid, better than what I imagined possible. I'd never seen a female drive the hay-wagon to the top of the mountain, so I had never imagined myself in that position.

I was nervous. This time there would be kids in the trailer instead of scrap concrete. The terrain had rocks and tight turns. It'd been almost half a year since I'd driven a big vehicle. To regain my confidence, my uncle took me for a practice run up the mountain and down. Because its front wheels turned, the trailer tracked better than the ones on the back of semis, so the turns didn't trouble me as much as I had expected. My uncle pointed out which rocks would jostle the passengers in the hay-wagon the most and told me to slow down going over them.

When we got back, a six-year-old boy sat with his grandmother in a golf cart. He looked at my uncle with big eyes and asked who would drive the hay-wagon.

My uncle smiled and pointed at me. "This one, right here! She's the most qualified."

A few minutes later, as the family got ready to climb into the hay-wagon, the little boy approached me with his wide eyes. "Um, can we, um, wait for my brother? Like, if—if . . . an hour, no, but—um, can we wait for him?"

"Where is he?"

"Up the hill."

"Yes, of course! Is he coming down? Do you know when? Would you like to go up and tell him to come down?"

"Yeah. Well, let's just say he's coming. We can wait?"

"Yes, we'll wait for your brother."

The boy had asked me as if I was in charge of the whole operation, as if I could've said no to waiting for his brother. He looked at me like I had the power, like I made the calls. If I'd said no, he wouldn't have argued, wouldn't have asked someone else. In his mind, my decision was final.

When we all got to the top of the mountain, my aunts gave me high-fives and called me an inspiration. They knew I was the youngest female to drive in the history of these hay-wagon rides and simply questioned whether I was the only female ever. But to me, I hadn't done it because I wanted to make a statement as a woman. I did it because I liked driving, because that's what I'd been professionally trained to do. I did it because that was my thing.

After praising me, my aunts went to set up dinner for everyone while I went to sit on a rock and drink sparkling water. Taking in the fresh air, I enjoyed the view of the valleys below. I could relax like the men had relaxed when I was a little girl. I didn't have to prove my worth anymore; I was the reason people got up here in the hay-wagon. One of the guests, who operated heavy machinery but did not hold a CDL, talked with me about how I have a CDL and how he'd recently taken up heavy machinery.

I'd grown used to the kind of attention I received from both my aunts and the older man. Women love that I'm a female "making history," and older men love having something interesting to talk about with me, especially since construction and CDL skills require dedication to obtain. I enjoy both, but another interaction on that mountain really hit my heart.

The same boy who had asked me to wait for his brother walked up to me again on the mountain. "Can we play tug-of-war?"

"Yeah!"

After my response, we both sat looking at each other. I wasn't sure why he was asking me permission. I wasn't his mother, and we weren't staying in the same house. I didn't really even know his name, but I could tell he was waiting expectantly for me to do something.

"Well, the rope is in the truck. . . ."

And that's when I understood. I was still master of the hay-wagon, even after we'd gotten to the top of the mountain. He could've asked any other adult to get the rope out for him, but he asked me because the hay-wagon was my domain. He'd directed both of his questions to me with more respect than I'd ever felt. I had the option to say no. I couldn't remember the last time I'd been asked a question where "no" was not only an acceptable answer but also somewhat expected. And then that's when it hit me: I never really wanted to be a truck driver at all. I just wanted respect.

Appendix

One big roadblock to my chosen career

Originally printed in the *Richmond Times-Dispatch* on September 17, 2018

I welcome a good challenge.

In an eighth-grade health class at St. Catherine's, we took a personality test to determine which career best suited us. My result: truck driver. This unusual result sparked a curiosity when passing semis on the highway or driving down the street. I actually started to wonder what it would take to become one. Of course, it wasn't a serious consideration, but I enjoyed the shock factor when responding to the classic "What do you want to be when you grow up?"

Then junior year at Maggie Walker, a classmate said, "Abi, be real. You're not really going to be a truck driver." Her comment spurred fantasy toward reality. Why couldn't I become a truck driver? What was the limiting factor? Societal pressures? Gender? Intelligence? Strength? Endurance? Aren't we trained from a young age that we can do anything we put our minds to?

To my classmate, I replied, "Watch me."

The week after graduating high school, I went to 7 Sons CDL Training to learn the necessary skills to obtain my license. I knew going in that it'd be tough, and throughout the course I shed a few tears. However, those frustrations only increased my desire to become a truck driver. My muscles strengthened, my confidence grew, and my emotional health stabilized. If I could parallel park an 18-wheeler, I could do anything.

To earn a commercial driver's license, I had to pass three written tests at the DMV: General Knowledge, Air Brakes, and Combination; identify parts of the truck for the pre-trip; master backing (straight back, offset, and parallel parking); and complete the road test, which included double-clutching on a 10-speed manual, turning with a 48-foot trailer, and general safe driving.

I passed those complicated tasks in mid-August and then encountered the limiting factor: my age. In Virginia, the CDL test requires a person to be 18, but a federal regulation prohibits anyone under 21 from driving trucks interstate. I'd assumed that, given the federal limitation, I could find a local, intrastate job, but due to insurance requirements, most demand over-the-road experience.

Then I came across the DRIVE-Safe Act (H.R. 5353/S. 3352), a bill moving through the U.S. House of Representatives and U.S. Senate that would allow 18- to 20-year-olds to drive across state lines with certain safety features installed in the vehicle and after completing 240 on-the-road hours with an experienced truck driver. This bill would replace the unnecessary restriction with more efficient ways to enhance road safety, especially in an economy where there is a massive truck driver shortage.

Mile and hour restrictions protect everyone on the road, but this age restriction is unhelpful. While drivers older than 21 are less likely to be involved in an accident, the required hours and tests that the bill sets forth increase driver experience and awareness to a degree that would substantially enhance safety, regardless of the trucker's age.

At 18 years old, I'm considered an adult. I'm expected to go to college or start my career. I'm trusted to make life-altering choices, and the possibilities for adults are virtually endless, except for this restriction. Despite my credentials, I'm having a tough time launching a professional truck-driving career.

I hope the Virginia delegation will support the DRIVE-Safe Act so that young Virginians can move on with their careers rather than be subject to an arbitrary waiting period.

Acknowledgments

*Everyone I have ever met shaped me into who I am
and therefore shaped this book into what it is.
Thank you.*

About the Author

Abigail was born and is living, unless she has died.

CPSIA information can be obtained
at www.ICGtesting.com
Printed in the USA
FSHW011514011120
75340FS